PRAISE FOR *THE IN-BETWEEN PLACE*

"My favorite books are the ones that feel applicable and directional— they meet me where I'm at, and then they point me to my friend and Savior, Jesus. *The In-Between Place* is just that, and Kat Armstrong is one of the truth-speaking, gracious, and honest guides that our genera- tion is craving right now. I want her to teach me the Bible and tell me stories. I also want to go to coffee with her. I can't help you get coffee with Kat, but I can encourage you to read this book and grab one for a friend. This is a gift."

— JESS CONNOLLY, AUTHOR OF *YOU ARE THE GIRL FOR THE JOB* AND
    TAKE IT TOO FAR

"Kat Armstrong is a true theologian. She represents a rising generation of women no longer content to simply receive the Word of God but commit- ted to lead, teach, mentor, and empower through a deeper understanding of his promises. Kat's ability to extract the layered nature of God as it weaves together the honesty of our story mesmerized me throughout the course of this entire book! With each page the eyes of my heart widened, and I saw myself there, at the well with the woman, together with all women throughout history—chosen and beloved by Jesus. I felt every human emotion while reading this superbly written, deeply personal book. Prepare yourself to trust God more through redemption you never thought possible! Like me, you will leave this book radically changed and ready to read it again!"

— KASEY VAN NORMAN, BESTSELLING AUTHOR OF *NOTHING WASTED*
    AND *NAMED BY GOD*

"You will find Kat Armstrong's book funny, introspective, bluntly honest about herself, gracious toward others, and an insightful journey into John's gospel. Her love for God, his Word, and women permeates the pages. It's refreshing."

— JOANN HUMMEL, LEAD TEACHING PASTOR OF BENT TREE BIBLE
    FELLOWSHIP

"Writing with the verve, clarity, and of mission that characterized the late Rachel Held Evans's best work, Kat Armstrong addresses the issue of what to do if one is caught betwixt and between—between anxiety and hope, between an old job and a new possibility, between sickness and health, and so much more. The focus of this study can be ably summed up in the words of Paul—'God works all things together for those who love him.' If indeed this is so, and Kat provides numerous compelling examples, including her own personal ones, then we should not be anxious but rather excited to see how things turn out, even if it involves suffering and loss along the way, because Jesus himself is not only with us all the way—he is the way into our future. I do not doubt this study will be especially helpful to professional Christian women whom Kat Armstrong has been ministering to for some time and who have to deal with constant challenges in the public sphere."

— BEN WITHERINGTON III, AMOS PROFESSOR OF NEW TESTAMENT FOR DOCTORAL STUDIES, ASBURY THEOLOGICAL SEMINARY

"Although 90 percent of the characters in the Bible are male, stories that feature women are deep wells of wisdom and instruction, moments when God's view of his daughters clashes sharply with how even the best human cultures view them. In her timely book, *The In-Between Place*, Armstrong delves deeply into the stories of Dinah, Jacob's only named daughter; the unnamed Samaritan woman who met Jesus at Jacob's well; and several others. Her search for answers from these women will fuel the faith and hope of readers stuck in an in-between place of grief, disappointment, hopelessness, and heartache."

— CAROLYN CUSTIS JAMES, AUTHOR OF *THE GOSPEL OF RUTH: LOVING GOD ENOUGH TO BREAK THE RULES* AND *FINDING GOD IN THE MARGINS*

"This is a delightful read! Kat generously shares stories from her own life alongside the story of the woman at the well in John 4 to demonstrate how Jesus meets us in our in-between places. Her book is empowering and full of hope."

— DR. CARMEN JOY IMES, ASSOCIATE PROFESSOR OF OLD TESTAMENT AT PRAIRIE COLLEGE IN THREE HILLS, ALBERTA; AUTHOR OF *BEARING GOD'S NAME: WHY SINAI STILL MATTERS*

"The Christian life is one long in-between space, between heaven and earth, the already and not yet. But sometimes the smaller in-betweens, such as between school and career, singleness and marriage, job and vocation, or overcoming past sins and living free, can feel overwhelming, irredeemable, or impassable. In *The In-Between Place*, Kat meets her readers where they are and points them to the power, mercy, and loving-kindness of Jesus Christ, who is with us in these places and who works mightily in and through them to his glory. Structuring her book around the story of Jesus meeting the Samaritan woman at the well in John 4, Kat gives us a biblical and theological framework to view our own stories and in-between places. As someone who feels like she has lived much of her life in in-between spaces, I wish I had had Kat's book fifteen years ago! Refreshing, personal, and Christ-centered, Kat's latest book will be sure to help many people in the in-between to live out in faith and confidence that Jesus is able to change their stories."

— KRISTEN PADILLA, AUTHOR OF *NOW THAT I'M CALLED: A GUIDE FOR WOMEN DISCERNING A CALL TO MINISTRY*

"As always, Kat empowers women through her words. With direct honesty and a solid biblical foundation, this book will make you want to run hard after Jesus. If you find yourself in an in-between place, Kat is the girl who will tell you the truth rather than let you flounder. Besides, who doesn't love the woman at the well and want to take the story to another level? This book is honest, smart, compassionate, and encouraging, just like Kat!"

— KATE MERRICK, AUTHOR OF *AND STILL SHE LAUGHS* AND *HERE, NOW*

"I've spent much of my life in in-between places—ones that have the effect of making me feel like an unmoored vessel floating in uncharted waters. So I love that Kat Armstrong has written a book dedicated to the in-between place, recognizing it as one where Jesus meets us and radically changes everything. Anchored in the story of a Samaritan woman's encounter with Jesus at a historically significant well in a spiritually significant place, the book is a work of theology in motion. Armstrong unpacks the life-changing implications of every part of this encounter through the delightful combination of humorous and serious storytelling, pop culture references, and rigorous but accessible biblical exegesis. It's relatable, encouraging, thought-provoking, and healing."

— JUDY WU DOMINICK, ESSAYIST

"There are few things I appreciate more than writers who are honest, vulnerable, and willing to give you a glimpse of the rawest parts of their stories, particularly from their own social locations. Kat does all of this and more in *The In-Between Place*, weaving her personal narrative alongside narratives of women in Scripture, even the hard ones that we often ignore or skip over. Focusing primarily on the Samaritan woman at the well, Kat offers in-depth exegesis and biblical interpretation in a way that is engaging and insightful. You'll surely walk away from this book drawn closer to the heart of God."

— KAT ARMAS, HOST OF THE PROTAGONISTAS PODCAST AND AUTHOR
OF *ABUELITA FAITH: WHAT WOMEN ON THE MARGINS TEACH US
ABOUT WISDOM, PERSISTENCE AND STRENGTH*

"Sometimes a place in the Bible's narrative becomes like a character with a voice of its own. Shechem/Sychar is such a place. Dinah was raped in this town, and Jesus met 'the woman at the well' here. In Kat Armstrong's book *The In-Between Place*, the author takes readers to this locale in Samaria and guides them through a literary, religious, and geographical look at how God has used this place and its people to reveal his sovereignty and grace. Armstrong's book is full of amusing anecdotes, astute observations, and life-changing applications. Highly recommended!"

— DR. SANDRA GLAHN, BIBLE TEACHER, PROFESSOR OF MEDIA ARTS
AND WORSHIP AT DALLAS THEOLOGICAL SEMINARY; AUTHOR OF
THE COFFEE CUP BIBLE STUDY SERIES

THE
IN-BETWEEN
PLACE

ALSO BY KAT ARMSTRONG

*No More Holding Back: Emboldening
Women to Move Past Barriers, See Their
Worth, and Serve God Everywhere*

THE
IN-BETWEEN
PLACE

WHERE JESUS CHANGES YOUR STORY

KAT ARMSTRONG

W Publishing Group

An Imprint of Thomas Nelson

Published in Nashville, Tennessee, by W Publishing, an imprint of Thomas Nelson.

Author is represented by the Christopher Ferebee Agency, www.christopherferebee .com.

Thomas Nelson titles may be purchased in bulk for educational, business, fundraising, or sales promotional use. For information, please email SpecialMarkets@ThomasNelson.com.

ISBN 978-0-7852-2351-1 (audiobook)
ISBN 978-0-7852-3447-4 (eBook)
ISBN 978-0-7852-2350-4 (TP)

Library of Congress Cataloging-in-Publication Data

Library of Congress Control Number: 2020944480

Printed in the United States of America

21 22 23 24 25 LSC 10 9 8 7 6 5 4 3 2 1

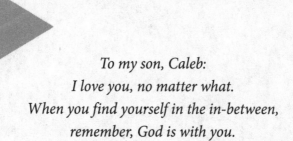

To my son, Caleb:
I love you, no matter what.
When you find yourself in the in-between,
remember, God is with you.

To my mom, Noemi:
Thank you for giving me the courage
I needed to finish this book.
My resilience comes from you.

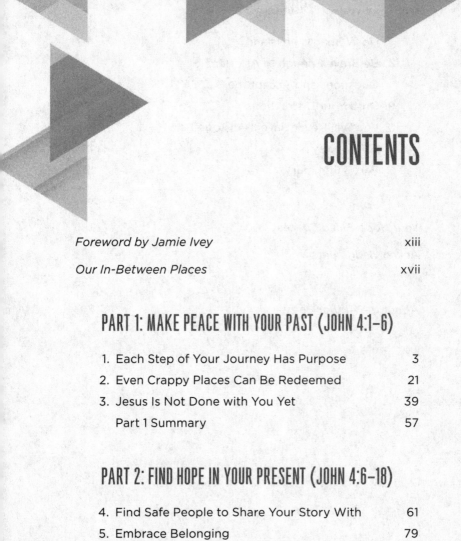

CONTENTS

Foreword by Jamie Ivey   xiii

Our In-Between Places   xvii

PART 1: MAKE PEACE WITH YOUR PAST (JOHN 4:1–6)

1. Each Step of Your Journey Has Purpose   3
2. Even Crappy Places Can Be Redeemed   21
3. Jesus Is Not Done with You Yet   39

    Part 1 Summary   57

PART 2: FIND HOPE IN YOUR PRESENT (JOHN 4:6–18)

4. Find Safe People to Share Your Story With   61
5. Embrace Belonging   79
6. Stop Showing Up for Yourself   95

    Part 2 Summary   113

CONTENTS

PART 3: STEP CONFIDENTLY INTO YOUR FUTURE (JOHN 4:16–41)

7. No Woman Is an Island   117

8. Be Brave Enough to Ask Hard Questions and Accept the Truth   133

9. Drop Your Distractions   149

10. You Will Never Have It All Together; Go Anyway   167

    Part 3 Summary   183

Your Hope-Filled Spaces   185

Acknowledgments   191

Notes   195

About the Author   203

FOREWORD

I have this dream of being an incredible gardener. I don't want a garden full of fancy flowers or exotic plants. No, I want a vegetable garden. I want a vibrant, organic, photo-worthy garden overflowing with vegetables to feed my family and to make some of my mom's famous homemade salsa. I picture myself strolling through rows of raised garden beds in a wide-brimmed hat and a cute half-apron that holds my garden scissors, carrying the most adorable basket that I keep filling with veggie after veggie. I want to grow every variety of tomato known to man. Bring on all of the peppers, onions, corn, squash, strawberries, melons—I want it all!

You should see my garden Pinterest board. There, the possibilities are endless! I pin photos and articles about the most beautiful gardens you've ever seen—gardens full of every vegetable known to humankind. I've saved all of the articles about building raised beds, the best home garden tools, and how to keep the wildlife out of my tomatoes.

The reality is that my actual garden looks nothing like this. There is no strolling with a basket. I don't have the wide-brimmed hat. The picture of the overflowing vegetable garden lives only in my mind. I haven't planned out my garden. I haven't bought all of the supplies. I haven't planted all of those plants. The garden in my yard looks nothing like my dream, because I haven't tended to the garden.

I want the fruit from the garden, but I haven't done any of the work.

I read an article[1] recently about a gardener named Timothy Tilghman, the head gardener at the gorgeous Untermyer Park and Gardens in Yonkers, NY. "If you can't enjoy weeding, you won't be a happy gardener," he said. "Everyone enjoys the neatness of a fresh planting, but unless you're willing and eager to get in there and weed . . ."

I stopped right there. That's it. That's me. I want the veggies, but I get frustrated with the weeds. I want the food for my family, but when it comes to digging in the dirt on a hot summer day, I bow out of the process and head to the grocery store. It's the in-between place of gardening that holds me back.

And yet, the more I think about those weeds, the more I realize that most of my life is spent in the weeds, in the space between where I was and where I'm going. I live between the planting of a dream and the realization of that dream. Between my wedding day and sitting in matching rocking chairs with gray hair. Between the birth of children and launching them into the world. Between Jesus saving us from our sin and dancing with him in glory forever.

I live in this place of not having arrived at where I'm going but knowing that I am closer than when I started. And it's in that in-between where I see my Jesus. It's in that in-between where Jesus comes right alongside me and is so close to me. It's in the weeds. In the in-between places. He always shows up in those places.

When I first started following Jesus, I had more baggage than an international cargo plane. I was afraid he would not really love me once he discovered the real me. (Come to find out, he knew the real me the whole time!) I was afraid that I would disappoint him—that I didn't have it in me to be a good Christian girl. And do you know what happened in those early years of following Jesus? He met me right where I was, and he and I walked through the weeds together. He was constantly pursuing me, loving me, and caring for me, just like he is still doing two decades later.

In these honest, heartfelt pages, my friend Kat points you to that same Jesus—the Jesus who meets us in the in-between. Jesus interrupts the life of the woman at the well the same way he interrupted mine. Jesus meets her in her in-between place, the same way he met me in mine. The pursuit, love, care, reconciliation that I experienced is the same that he pours out on her.

We all have dreams. But we don't always know how to get there. Sometimes we just feel stuck. Sometimes we don't know if we're worthy of being unstuck. Jesus knows your dreams and your fears. And he's not afraid to get down in the dirt with you or spend time with you in the weeds—in the places we spend so much of our lives. Kat knows this Jesus well. She walks with him, she talks with him, and her greatest desire in life is for you to know him too.

My desire for you, friend, as you turn the pages of this beautifully written book, is that you would see Jesus with you, in your in-between places—and not just your in-between places now, but also the in-between places of your past—and know with full confidence that when you reach another in-between place (and I'm certain you will) he will meet you there as well.

Open your heart to all that Jesus has to offer. He's worth it every single time.

Jamie Ivey
Author of *You Be You: Why Satisfaction
and Success Are Closer Than You Think*
Host of *The Happy Hour with Jamie Ivey*
podcast

OUR IN-BETWEEN PLACES

"I don't ever want to come back here again."

In the middle of the night, Aaron and I dragged ourselves across the parking lot of Baylor Hospital Dallas and toppled into the car. As seat belts were clicked and gears shifted into reverse, my body felt feeble—one nudge and I'd melt into a puddle of tears—but my tone of voice carried notes of unrelenting determination. We had just said good-bye to my father for the last time.

For the last two weeks, his ICU room had officially become my in-between place. I had found myself stuck in between his life and his death.

Known as Ron, Ronald, or Ronnie, my dad suffered with a lifetime of substance abuse and depression. In his last few years, a spine injury left him in chronic pain and stole his will to live. Before he passed, he spent several weeks in the intensive care unit after trying to shoot himself in the heart. The wounds he inflicted upon himself eventually took his life. The tragic irony was that he missed his heart but shattered all of ours.

The social worker, who sat with me and my mom after Dad was admitted to the hospital, tried to explain how radically our lives had been turned upside down, but the shock of it all numbed me to her words. She spoke a language I understood, and yet I couldn't process one word coming out of her mouth. Without knowing what tomorrow would bring, I tried unsuccessfully to grasp that life as we knew it was a thing of the past. Even if my dad survived, which seemed unlikely from the doctor's point of view, he didn't want to live. This in-between place was one for my dad too. What would he do with a second chance? Would he take it?

Feeling as though we were on a terrifying roller coaster, our family rode the highs and lows of each day's medical updates. We were strapped in tight but dangling from death-defying heights while the ride clicked slowly up a steep incline, and all the while, we knew that a neck-whipping, ear-flapping downward spiral was imminent. He survived a surgery. We had hope. He took a turn for the worse, so we prepared to say good-bye. He made it through the night, and we rallied to pray for a miracle. He'd wake up and swear he wanted to live; the next moment he would fall asleep mumbling about how much he wanted to see Jesus.

On one visit I came to the hospital intending to kneel down next to his bed and pray. My grand plan included petitioning God for healing, declaring verses of peace and comfort over the room with bold confidence, then reading aloud to my father from Psalm 23, a chapter in the Bible about God's tender care and protection when we feel like we are in the valley of the shadow of death. I was going to speak against evil forces with 2 Corinthians 1, which names God "the God of all comfort" (v. 3). But I didn't even make it into his room. I ended up paralyzed in the hallway, unable to push open the door. Peering through the window, holding the station nurse's hand, was the best I could do. Next thing I knew, I was riding the elevator up and down with strangers, sobbing in the corner and staring at the elevator buttons, wishing there were some sort of eject button to get me out of the nightmarish reality.

Thank God for Baylor's chaplaincy program and for the compassionate nurses. The prayers offered for me and my family by the chaplains on call ministered to us in a way I hadn't experienced before. But I hope I never have to meet another hospital chaplain in an intensive care room. I'll never forget the gentleness and dignity with which one of my father's nurses explained what to expect when you remove care and wait for someone's last breath. She has all my respect and admiration, but I don't want to have to see her again. Thank God for the nurses stationed in rooms for round-the-clock suicide watch. But I'm sure you can understand why I could barely look them in the eye when I hugged them on the way in and out of my dad's room.

The smells, the sounds, the beeps of machines . . . it was all too much, honestly. I regret not visiting him more. And that just can't be undone now.

Even now, I don't want to think about that hospital room,

I don't want to see it ever again, and I wouldn't wish that in-between space on an enemy. But it is not my only brush with feeling stuck; it is just by far the most severe.

I, like the rest of you, know what it is like to watch the president of the United States give a daily press briefing about COVID-19, the global pandemic impacting our whole world, and wonder how we will face tomorrow. It feels like an in-between place. How are we supposed to plan for the future when we don't know what the next day will bring?

In a less intense, almost incomparable way, many seasons of my life have felt suspended in frustration, fear, and insecurity because I had a clear goal and fell short of it. I knew the direction I was headed but never seemed to arrive. Carmen Joy Imes, a professor of Old Testament at Prairie College, describes the phenomenon as knowing "what you're cut out to do, but you can't get the traction you need to get there."[1]

While pandemics and losing a parent are a part of my story, this book isn't really about those things. It's about threshold moments, big and small, that sometimes turn into transitional or even tragic seasons of life. If you're not in one now, you likely just came out of one, or at some point you'll be in the middle of what feels like nowhere. And you'll ask questions like these:

How did I end up here?

Why can't I seem to move on?

Why do I feel stuck, and how do I change?

Is this as good as it gets?

How do I make the most of this sucky season?

Maybe you are paralyzed by fear right now; some looming

decision has you unable to make the next right step. Maybe you are peering through a metaphorical window into your future, wishing you had the confidence—the courage, really—to open the doors. You know you have to face reality to experience progress, but you just can't find the resilience to do so. Maybe you feel as if your life is an elevator: you push all the right buttons, the doors open and close as usual, and everyone else seems to get off on the right floor in their relationships and careers, but you are stuck in the corner looking for an eject button. You just want out. Or maybe every assumption you made about your life feels as though it was proved wrong overnight. This is exactly how I felt the weeks my dad was in the ICU.

In God's providence, Baylor Hospital Dallas is a block away from Dallas Theological Seminary, which I often frequent for happy reasons—like learning more about Jesus, meeting with mentors, or getting lost in the book stacks. In spite of the instructions from my map app that tries to send me on a different route, now I choose to drive by the hospital on the way to the seminary for the sake of remembering. While I bound up the stairs at Turpin Library, eager to find my next book, I sense grief lurking nearby. Who can make sense of the intermingling of joy and sorrow in this life?

Seems to me, in our in-between places—in between jobs, in between kids, in between our hopes and dreams and the cruelty of real life, in between sickness and health, in between confusion and clarity, in between divorce and remarriage, in between the ICU and death, in between the cross and the new heaven and new earth—hopelessness often pitches a tent. When we feel overlooked and forgotten, when we can't find answers, when we don't understand how we got *here*, when life doesn't make sense, when we don't know who we are anymore, when the best we can do is turn off the lights, crawl into bed, and hope we don't wake up tomorrow, *that's* when we need Jesus to redeem our in-between places. And I'm convinced he can. He has. And he will do it again. This time, for you.

BETWEEN A ROCK AND A HARD PLACE

Life is a journey designed to help us move forward into the goodness God has planned for us, but if we feel like we are in a holding pattern (or our place in life sucks), it's easy to fall into a pit of self-pity—or worse, despair—especially with the tent of hopelessness darkening our view. If you are there now, I have good news for you. Although you might not be able to see your way out, and your determination might have been knocked out of you in your fall, Jesus can climb into that pit with you and lift you up with *his* mighty power. You don't even have to make the first move; he will. I know this because of a conversation recorded in John 4 that Jesus had with the Samaritan woman at the well while he was on his way from Judea to Galilee.

Some of you know you got yourself into the mess and think you should at least be the person to get yourself out.

Some of you might be thinking that your holding pattern wasn't even your fault. Someone else's mistakes put you there. They are the ones who need to get help. But their sins are weighing you down and keeping you from moving forward.

Some of you might feel powerless to change your circumstances, fated to a future beyond your control.

No matter your entry point, come with me on this journey following Jesus from Judea, a place where his ministry was taking off, to Galilee, his comfortable home base. If you're longing for the days when all was right in the world—or at the very least, predictable—that might be your Judea. If you're longing for a bright future because you know once you get there, everything's going to pan out, that might be your Galilee. In between Jesus' departure from Judea and his destination in Galilee, he traveled through Samaria, a broken place everyone knew to avoid. In the region of Samaria, Jesus purposely stopped in a town called Sychar, which is another name for Shechem.[2]

It's really tempting to tune out the name of a place that is ancient and unfamiliar. But the message of *The In-Between Place* centers on Shechem, a location you'll find only on an ancient map. Its historical significance in the biblical narrative is impossible to ignore, though easy to underestimate. I can't wait to guide you on this discovery process. I believe you are going to find hope—inestimable hope.

Hope is not like motivation or inspiration, fleeting and unpredictable, and hope is not like the promise of a new job or access to a vaccine. Hope, *real hope*, is certainty that a loving God will come from outside our circumstances, enter into our messy reality, and be with us through it all as he works everything out for our good.

Following Jesus' travels in John 4, we will see for ourselves that what we once condemned as a place we did not want to go, let alone hang out for a while, can be the location of our most hope-filled encounters with our Savior. If the Samaritan woman's conversation with Jesus teaches us anything, it's that sometimes Jesus saves our greatest spiritual breakthroughs for our in-between places in life. Trouble is, I'm usually not hoping for a sacred conversation with Jesus. I'm wishing I could go back in time and choose another path so I wouldn't end up in the same place, or I just want him to get me out. Learning to deal ranks far second to deliverance.

The In-Between Place is for all of us who can't see a way forward. It is for the person who feels that if she looks left, her face will be scraped by an immovable boulder, and if she looks right, she'll see nothing but hard to handle. It's for the person who feels lost and is not sure she is worth the effort to be found. And it's for the person whose life is actually good right now but who is supporting loved ones and friends through really hard things.

I'm in an in-between place now. I'm not writing as one who's arrived. Ten feet underground, I'm peering up from a pit of anxiety, straining to see if anyone can hear my calls for help.

Besides my seventeen years as Aaron Armstrong's wife, there's no title, role, or position I've held long enough for it to become a part of me the way leading Polished Ministries has been grafted into my DNA. For twelve years I've served as the cofounder and executive director of this ministry, which gathers professional women to help them navigate their careers and explore their faith. It has profoundly shaped my understanding of who I am—or at least who I think I am—which makes any future succession planning terrifying. Soon I'll drop the title *executive director* and pass the baton to someone who will help us reach our fullest potential. Who am I beyond being known as the leader of the ministry I helped birth? Will there still be a "me" when someone replaces me as executive director and the only part of my title that remains is cofounder? When the ministry spreads across the world, which I believe it will, will I still feel a part of it? Does my part even matter?

So, trust me—if you're staring down uncertainty or confusion, you are not alone. Your rock and a hard place might be a transition at work, or perhaps you've been homeschooling your children but have determined the best for them is in public school, so now your last few years don't make sense or add up. Why all the planning and preparation and confidence in what seemed to be God's will if you have to change directions so radically?

Maybe you feel stuck in the swell of dark emotions that follow a bad breakup, a messy divorce, a loveless relationship, or an abusive spouse. Or any number of other circumstances that throw a wrench in your dreams and plans, like infertility, adultery, postpartum depression, or retirement. Maybe your place of business is shutting down overnight or your main source of income is drying up.

Internal confusion, too, can be an in-between place. It's decades spent in an industry that no longer welcomes you or feels safe. It's a lifetime of pouring into your family and their not appreciating your sacrifices. Whatever it is, it's all too real—but hold off on giving up hope until you hear the story of Jesus and the Samaritan woman.

HOW JESUS CHANGES OUR STORIES

In the following chapters we're going to dig into the paradox of confusing, frustrating, and sometimes hopeless circumstances that position us to experience God's love with unexplainable spiritual breakthroughs. We're going to learn how Jesus changes our stories even if our circumstances remain the same.

After careful study, I've come to the conclusion that Jesus' conversation with the Samaritan woman at the well teaches us how we can make peace with our past, so I've focused on that in part 1 of this book. In part 2, we will learn how to find hope in our present, knowing that Jesus redeems every season of our lives. And in part 3, we will learn how we can be empowered to step confidently into our future. I've organized *The In-Between Place* so each chapter unpacks a few verses in John 4. In every chapter I'll do three things: (1) help you understand what is happening in that passage of Scripture, (2) highlight one way Jesus changes our stories, and (3) explore how we can apply that truth to our lives. Along the way, I'll debunk some common misconceptions about the woman at the well—namely, that she was a prostitute. She wasn't.

I want to encourage you to read this book with at least one other person, if not a small group. God does special things when we process with trusted friends. That's why I've included discussion questions at the end of each chapter to help guide your conversations. Nothing would bring me more joy as a Bible teacher than to encourage your interest in the Bible. My life's goal is to get our generation to look again at the Scriptures with holy curiosity. Additionally, I've concluded each chapter with a link to a place on my website where you can download a free study guide and a video. You'll find helpful articles, illustrations, and sources for anyone who wants to dig a little deeper in the study guide. I pray it is a help to you and your friends.

However you plan to use the book, I want you to know the rug in my office has often been soaked with my tears and imprinted with two worn-down patches big enough for my knees, as I position myself to ask God to do something through this message only he can do. I've pestered him, begged him to lift words off pages and flood your life with hope. By God's grace; the life, death, and resurrection of Jesus; and the power of the Holy Spirit, my prayer is that this book will usher in the kind of spiritual revival we dared not believe was possible. Your doubts, fears, track record, mistakes, bad decisions, and insecurities are no match for God. You and I might feel lost, but hope isn't. He's making his way to us now.

No more sleepless nights speculating over past decisions; no more insecurities driving us into the ground; no more holding back on moving forward into our callings. No more.

PART ONE

MAKE PEACE
WITH YOUR PAST

Now when Jesus learned that the Pharisees had
heard, "Jesus is making and baptizing more disciples
than John"—although it was not Jesus himself but his
disciples who baptized—he left Judea and started
back to Galilee. But he had to go through Samaria. So
he came to a Samaritan city called Sychar, near the
plot of ground that Jacob had given to his son Joseph.
Jacob's well was there, and Jesus, tired out by his journey, was sitting by the well. It was about noon.

—JOHN 4:1-6 NRSV

ONE

EACH STEP OF YOUR JOURNEY HAS PURPOSE

God has a master plan for our lives.

—REVEREND PEGGY R. SCOTT

In between a lucrative few years as one of the youngest skin-care consultants in Arbonne International, a growing network marketing company, and cofounding Polished, a national non-profit ministry to professional women, I found myself answering phones at a laundry company for college students. Not exactly the stepping-stone I envisioned after leaving a season of success and planning for an upcoming season of impact. But there I was, asking frustrated customers if they would mind holding while I tried to catch the rolling calls headed for the company voice mail.

Picture me, chained to my desk and squished into a headset, answering calls from unhappy customers who wanted to talk to someone in charge. While I discussed the pilling on yoga pants, the stains on sorority formal outfits, or the price comparisons on dry cleaning, I was wishing I'd never left Arbonne International leadership and was praying that Polished Ministries would become more than just a dream. During my first few years at the laundry company, I'd regularly wake my husband in the middle of the night with what he called "dream-induced gibberish," until he realized I was saying, "University Laundry, this is Kat. How can I help you?"

I learned invaluable professional and spiritual lessons at University Laundry—as a customer service rep, then office manager, and then a catchall for the CEO. I learned lessons about teamwork, using my work as a way to honor God, and leading from the middle. But at the time, the education and experience I received on this job felt purposeless.

With perfect hindsight, I thank God I had a role in the company in a season of rapid expansion. Later I would need that experience to guide me as Polished chapters started up in states outside our Texas incorporation. Listening in on conference calls between University Laundry's CEO and university administration, just for the purpose of taking notes, became training ground for calls with churches interested in partnering with Polished to bring a chapter to their city. But at the time, I felt lost and often asked myself and my friends, "What am I doing here? Where is all of this going?"

Have you ever felt frozen in time while everyone else seems to be moving ahead at Mach speed? Like you're the only one who's crashed on some turn in life while the rest of the crowd speeds through detours like future thought-leaders and experts? The feeling is mutual and, I think, universal. Using text messages to poll my friends, I asked if anyone else had experienced feeling stuck—like there was no way out of their current situation and it didn't make one ounce of sense how their family/work/church happenings were unfolding. Turns out, *everyone* in my life feels stuck, at least in some form or fashion. Most expressed the hopelessness that shadows dead-end jobs, relationships, or ministry opportunities. Singles, marrieds, mothers (both single and married), widows, divorcées, stay-at-home moms, gig-economy workers, corporate executives—*all* the women I asked, even the ones "running in their lane," mentioned their struggles with decision fatigue, the feeling of being overwhelmed when barraged by constant decision making. Being in their sweet spot didn't disqualify them from feeling stuck either. It wasn't the same type of stuckness my confused and weary friends mentioned, but the I-haven't-arrived sentiment echoed in 100 percent of my conversations.

Every single person who confided in me asked, "Is there something wrong with me?" As if being hard-pressed was evidence that there was. They described themselves as *dumb, insignificant, lost, beyond help, a train wreck out of options and prospects. Whoosh.*

This is where my tendency to challenge comes into play. I've got to push back on these assumptions. Being stuck is normal because you are not a robot. You are a human. Part of being human is living through unwanted and unexpected change, wading through confusion, and persevering through seasons you wish were much shorter. Although my group of friends expressed concern that their in-between places corresponded with their deficiencies—a lie I wholeheartedly rejected—another pattern emerged. The whole lot of us testified to supernatural experiences with God in the middle of testing times.

Like it or not, some of our most meaningful, memorable, and life-changing moments in relationship with God are reserved for our in-between places. Where we feel most pinned down or tied up can be a sacred space for God to hold our attention while he holds our hands. There is God-redeemed purpose in every part of our stories, and God is working all things for our good. We might understand that these are core tenets of the Christian faith, but they are so hard to believe. It takes practice to believe what we know is true. That means you and I will become more acquainted with time-is-standing-still-but-I-want-out feelings before our time on earth is complete. That's not a new emotion, as we can see in Scripture.

John, the beloved disciple of Jesus and eyewitness to Jesus' life, death, and resurrection, included in his gospel account the story about Jesus traveling to Samaria, that region of Israel stuck between Judea and Galilee. Judea, Samaria, and Galilee were generally considered in Roman times to be the three main geographical divisions of Palestine.[1] In his gospel, John brings our attention to a conversation between a Samaritan woman at a well in Sychar (remember this is also known as Shechem) because it's paramount to John's retelling of history. It was a conversation John wouldn't have overheard firsthand, so he might have spent a considerable amount of time talking with the Samaritan woman himself to get the story straight.

Before we get to the words exchanged between the woman at the well and Jesus, our Savior, it's important, crucial even, that we see there was a purpose in all the stops Jesus made as he traveled. You see, Jesus never makes any move that isn't part of his plan. As we follow Jesus' footsteps to Samaria, a place where a lot of people ended up between a rock and a hard place, we will find that he helped a woman make peace with her past. When you feel like you are in no-man's-land, or no-woman's-land, drifting aimlessly, ready yourself. A Savior is coming to Samaria.

PURPOSE IN THE PLAN

In a remarkable feat of cunning and self-control, I hid my pregnancy from Aaron for ten weeks. By the time he found out, I was past my first trimester and had visited the doctor twice. Having prepared an answer for anything that could tip him off, I was able to keep him in the dark about my changing body, moodiness, and new eating habits, even though he called them to my attention. I told him my breasts looked bigger due to a new push-up bra. I said they'd really come a long way in technology, and my bustline was going to be super impressive moving forward. *Lies.* I assured him that my new eating habits corresponded with my workout program. Little did he know I was on the eat-everything-in-sight meal plan that aligned with my walk-at-a-snail's-pace workout regimen.

When he commented about my moodiness, I whipped back that menstruating was hard and he should tread lightly. Aaron also didn't know I was leaving work at two o'clock every day to go home and sleep for three extra hours, then waking up to an alarm to reapply my makeup and pretend I had just arrived home at the same time he did so he wouldn't notice the plummet in my energy level. That would have been a dead giveaway.

Why all the secrecy? After the pee stick confirmed we were going to have a baby, mystified, I looked at the calendar to try and determine conception, only to realize that our ten-year wedding anniversary was ten weeks away. Since our celebration trip was already planned, I wondered if I could conceal the surprise to make for an epic ten-year anniversary present. When I pitched my ob-gyn the idea to wait two and a half months to tell my husband I was pregnant, she snort-laughed. She said it was unlikely I could pull that off, which sounded like a challenge to me. I left her office determined to prove her wrong and to secure wife-of-the-year status, with pictures as a trophy. My next call was to a photographer. Besides my ob-gyn, the photographer was the only person in my life who knew I was pregnant before Aaron. Then I began devising a grand plan to capture the moment I told Aaron we were going to have a baby.

Right before we left for our trip, I casually mentioned to Aaron that I had booked a photographer to take some anniversary pictures. He scoffed. Why would we spend money on a professional if all we wanted was a few shots of us at the restaurant? I assured him to trust me; we would want these photos forever, and they needed to be frame-worthy. Although we had agreed to no presents, I joked that I did have a present for him, but not to worry, I didn't buy it. It was homemade. *Wink*. One of his eyebrows practically broke away from his forehead and jumped up onto his bald head, because ten years of marriage had proved to Aaron that I'm not the homemaking type.

A week before leaving, I wrapped a set of three matching gift tins. The first, labeled "First comes love," had a framed picture of us at our engagement. The second, labeled "Then comes marriage," had a framed picture of our wedding. The third, labeled "Then comes a baby in a baby carriage," had a framed picture of the baby's sonogram. Aaron didn't put it together until the very last box. While the photographer snapped pictures of him opening box one, Aaron snickered, "Thanks, babe, for the picture *I already own*." By box two he was completely confused. He then began apologizing to the photographer for coming all the way out to the booking, saying, "I didn't know my wife was going to make such a big deal of things." *Shade*. The images of Aaron weeping over Caleb's first picture will forever rank as the most important pictures we own. The plan was a success.

We cried, embraced, kissed, and got it all on camera, thanks to my "making such a big deal of things." The only thing we could talk about at our candlelit dinner that evening was the future Caleb Armstrong. Together we replayed every single moment of the past ten weeks. Aaron started putting the pieces together; everything was starting to make sense.

Throughout the night I joked with Aaron that he should have trusted me about the photographer. After all, I had a plan. Every move was calculated and fit together to bring about this big reveal. He regretted poking fun at me and admitted he never saw this coming. To which I replied, "I know. We have pictures to memorialize your surprise."

Behind each part of my plan was a desire to show Aaron how much I loved him. I wonder if God feels similarly toward us, and if the purposes behind all Jesus' travels, conversations, healings, and revelations fit together in a way that brings him glory and works for our good.

What if each step in our journey has purpose? We know it does, don't we? That's not to say God causes bad things to happen to us. He's a good God, and all good things come from him. But he is able to take a good thing, like my pregnancy, or a really hard thing, like the death of my father, and bring joy from them both. We can look back at every point in our lives and see he was at work the whole time. But in the heat of the moment, when we feel like we are on fire, God says he can make beauty from the ashes that will be left over. So what if we dared to trust him more while we are in the midst of the flames? What if we viewed every single move Jesus makes as a move toward more complete redemption? That's what John's gospel does for us in his account: it helps us see the purpose of Jesus' movements.

It would be easy to skim over John's location markers in the story about the woman at the well, but if we are convinced that God is trustworthy, Jesus is moving with purpose, and all things are ultimately aligning for our good, we have to notice what happened right before and after his interaction with the woman at the well.

Before Jesus arrived in Samaria, he left Judea, where his conversation with the Pharisee, Nicodemus, took place.

According to John 3, Nicodemus was the opposite of the Samaritan woman in every possible way. He was a Jewish man, a religious leader, formally trained in theology and considered an authority on matters of the Jewish faith. The woman at the well, on the other hand, was obviously a woman in a man-led world, but also a Samaritan, and was nothing close to a religious leader or a person with any form of authority. Nicodemus's conversation with Jesus happened in private at night and ended in unbelief, whereas the woman's conversation with Jesus happened in private during the day and ended with her own profession of faith, as well as many in her city believing Jesus, too, because of her testimony. It's as if John organized his gospel account so that his readers would catch the contrast between Nicodemus and the woman at the well. Two strikingly different people in two radically different places with polar opposite responses to Christ.

I wonder how much peace we would experience if we looked back on some of the seasons we felt most stuck and compared them to the before-and-after. Would we see contrasts that open our eyes to God's work in our lives? I think so. If I were a betting woman, I'd wager you and I have work to do to make peace with our pasts, and it will require looking back not with regret or nostalgia but for the purpose of reflecting and assessing.

Before we review Jesus' words to the woman at the well, let's also think about what happened after Jesus left her presence. What was next on his journey? A trip to Galilee. Based on John 4:45, when Jesus arrived in Galilee, he had a warm reception. Which makes me think of Kelly Clarkson.

A few miles from my home is a small town called Burleson, Texas. I'm not sure if they still have the sign up, but after Kelly Clarkson won on *American Idol* and rose to fame as a pop singer, Burleson put up a sign that signaled to every visitor that they were in Kelly's hometown.

Much as Burleson is known as Kelly Clarkson's hometown, Galilee was known as Jesus' home base for ministry. Bible scholar Henry W. Holman compiled a list of many of the Jesus-related happenings in Galilee that I think you need to see.[2] Jesus grew up in Galilee, and so did eleven of his twelve apostles. (Judas was the exception. He was from Judea.) Most of Jesus' parables (nineteen of thirty-two) were spoken in Galilee, and the vast majority of his miracles (twenty-five of thirty-three) were performed there too. Some would contend that Galilee was where Jesus received the greatest response to his ministry. Both the Sermon on the Mount, one of the longest and best-known sermons of Christ, and the Lord's transfiguration happened in Galilee. Many of the women who followed Christ and ministered to him also came from there (Matt. 27:55). And two of Christ's most significant postresurrection appearances took place in Galilee (Matt. 28:16–20; John 21:1–23).

Sensing it was time to move on, Jesus left Judea to go to Galilee, but before he arrived, Jesus had the history-making conversation with a nameless woman at a Samaritan well. Thousands of years later it still captures our attention through John's retelling of the story. The way John positioned the story, in between a conversation with a curious religious elite named Nicodemus and the welcoming reception of the Galileans, should signal to us, the readers, that there is purpose in this stop.

Friend, Jesus hasn't forgotten you. If you are looking back with longing or ahead with caution, Jesus is with you—between jobs, between kids, between relationships. Feeling stuck is not a result of your not being good enough; it's the by-product of being a human. Thankfully, we don't need to muster up more faith or good works to move forward. Jesus does that work for us in *his* power.

PATHWAY TO TRUTH AND CHANGE

Had I been one of Jesus' original disciples, I think I would have encouraged him to stay in Judea. Not only was his ministry growing, his teaching was changing lives and catching the attention of the power players in the area, like Nicodemus. Things we work hard to do in our modern age. But the unusually high number of baptisms caught the Pharisees' attention, and that "success" is exactly why Jesus journeyed from Judea to Samaria.

But if he had to go, I would have encouraged him to move quickly through the region of Samaria. Instead, Jesus stopped in an area that was "in hostile tension with its Jewish neighbors" because of their differing views about the Messiah.[3] Samaria, the capital of the Northern Kingdom of Israel in the Old Testament, had a woeful backstory.[4] The prophet Isaiah devoted a significant portion of his prophetic chastisement to the people living there (Isa. 28). Isaiah condemned the Samaritans for being drunkards and painted a picture of the priests and prophets—supposedly the people most devoted to God—as stumbling around under the influence. He described all their tables as being covered in vomit, the stench marking the whole area. Samaritans were people who were stuck in horrible conditions, hated by their Jewish neighbors, and rebelling against God himself. The prophet Amos also called out Samaria by describing it as full of "great turmoil," defined by "acts of oppression" and people "incapable of doing right" (Amos 3:9–10).

Eek.

Ironically, in the New Testament, Samaria would become a gateway to the gospel's spread across the world. Dr. Luke, one of Jesus' disciples, quoted Jesus as saying that after his followers received the Holy Spirit, they would be his "witnesses in Jerusalem, in all Judea and Samaria, and to the ends of the earth" (Acts 1:8). Apparently for Christianity to spread, it would have to go through Samaria. What was once considered a place no Jew would be caught dead in—something we will talk more about soon—suddenly became the path for life and freedom from sin.

If we stretch our metaphor and use Samaria to represent the places we feel stuck in, maybe Samaria is also a funnel of truth and change.

My friend Angie gave a talk at a women's gathering I'll never forget. She hand-painted a piece of art that now hangs in my office with the three points of her message:

God has a plan, only he knows.
Push through the mess.
Eyes on him.

I'm grateful for the visual reminder that helps me return to those phrases when I am afraid, frustrated, or down.

Angie is living proof that God has a plan only he knows. When the opportunity presents itself, Angie is quick to share with women the twists and turns of her career. After suffering through rejection and disappointment, she speaks with conviction and fortitude about pushing through the messy parts of our lives by keeping our eyes on Jesus. He's the one who comes to us when we feel stuck. Give Angie a few minutes of your time, and you'll start to hear about her God, who graciously taught her life lessons through layoffs and extended seasons of unemployment. She'll be the first to tell you she may not have received these lessons had she not been positioned in total dependence upon his provision.

Similarly, the friends I polled via text about stuckness sounded as if they had all coordinated their stories behind the scenes, because, as I mentioned, all of them expressed, without prompting, the important lessons learned through their hardships. For one friend, it meant accepting her addiction to the approval of others and breaking free from the weight of people-pleasing. For another, it meant diving into relationships with more commitment and practicing gratitude to hold on to hope. Although her most recent season of feeling stuck could have been marked with bitterness, she learned to hope for a better future while asking God to sustain her.

In every response, there was a thread of hope. That thread was not a silver lining; some of the rocks and hard places in their lives were still painful or a result of a broken world, but their measure of hope had increased in spite of the situation, and perhaps because of it. And my friends attributed this to Jesus. Not to their own strength but to his. Not to their own glory, but to *his*.

We can't deny the obvious fact that places like Samaria are primed for the gospel to make a difference because the people living there need Jesus in more overt ways. Maybe this is why the woman at the well was so receptive to the truths Jesus taught her. Maybe the desperation we feel in our in-between places is not only a normal part of our humanity but also a sacred space for a deeper connection with Christ. Inasmuch as suffering is a natural part of being human, so is knowing God more intimately in those seasons of trial. Time will tell, but I think it's safe to assume that once we go through something terribly hard, we are better equipped to handle the next struggle. It's partly because we've experienced God's faithfulness, and we are more practiced at believing he has a good plan for us.

You and I could miss an opportunity to grow closer to God during our in-between stages. We can grumble our whole way through, throw a tantrum, and despise every minute we're stuck. Or we could continue to ask God to move us forward into a new season while at the same time asking him to show us what he wants us to learn right now. We could remind ourselves daily that there is purpose in his plan. We could journal about our fears and then tell God we're ready for him to give us hope. Because every single detour from our well-laid plans is an opportunity to embrace our need for God. Who knows, maybe something he reveals to you in your in-between season will be the guiding force of the rest of your life.

HERE WE GO AGAIN

On my last day at University Laundry, my pregnant belly brushed against my desk as I packed up my favorite G2 pens. I'd happily leave the place in better condition than I found it, but no one could take *my precious* (whispered in a Gollum voice) G2 pens. The owners and I still have a hard time remembering my exact start date, so we estimate I was employed with them for approximately six years. Thanks to a closetful of journals spilling over old boxes, I have proof that over the course of my six years serving the organization, I had experienced several spiritual victories.

During that season I led a small group of women through the book of Hebrews and discovered that if I could teach the Bible, no matter what else was happening in life, I would find joy. I cofounded Polished Ministries with my friend Stephanie Giddens and learned that no job title could take away from my assignment to serve women. And I sat under Dr. Glenn Kreider's teaching at Dallas Theological Seminary and understood grace more fully. If you turned my life into a chart, these three revelations would be high points.

Some of my most meaningful experiences with God happened during my in-between seasons of life when I felt most stuck in my career. Begging God to show me the way and having my heart attuned to his leading was the result of needing him more than I'd ever needed him before.

Weeks before that last day, my replacement was chosen, and I had the honor of training him in my responsibilities. The baton passing felt right and honorable and healthy—until we had to change desks. Passing on my knowledge and wisdom made me feel useful, but then came time for us to change places so that his physical position in the office reflected his place in the organization. It bruised my ego. I'd come so far and grown up so much, and rolling my desk chair in front of a new cubby felt like a step in the wrong direction. With one foot out the door and my monthlong notice almost complete, it was only normal to hire, train, and empower the next leader. Plus, I was moving on to devote more time to Polished, my passion project and new full-time job. I was starting to realize that my ideas of departures, in-between places, and destinations were wrong. Truth is, life is one long journey until we are home in Jesus' presence.

In the same way I eventually made peace with my past at University Laundry, I'm trying to live a life that is at peace with all the high and low points in my journey. I want to live a life grounded in these truths: feeling stuck is normal because I am human, and no matter where I end up, Jesus will come and find me when I feel lost.

John wrote that Jesus "had" to travel through Samaria, but the thing is, he didn't. At least not in the usual way we interpret the word *had* to mean "had no choice." Jesus made a deliberate choice. His destination, Samaria, would lead to a sacred conversation that would have redemptive impact on all of us.

Discussion Questions

1. Why do you think some of the most meaningful moments in our faith come during our in-between seasons?

2. Describe a time when you felt lost in life.

3. Describe a time when you felt found in Christ.

4. What kind of life circumstances make you feel alone in your struggles?

5. What does it mean to you that Jesus comes to be with us when we feel stuck?

6. What keeps you from trusting all God has planned for your life?

Study Guide

Visit www.katarmstrong.com/theinbetweenplace to download the free study guide and videos. Materials for chapter 1 include

- a map of Samaria
- a few pictures of Kat surprising Aaron

TWO

EVEN CRAPPY PLACES CAN BE REDEEMED

To be a Christian is to live every day of our
lives in solidarity with those who sit in darkness
and in the shadow of death, but to live in the
unshakable hope of those who expect the dawn.

—REVEREND FLEMING RUTLEDGE

I'm not in a good place. My life is crap, *quite literally*!

This text message bubbled into my friends' phones as I
pounded my forehead against my car steering wheel. My bes-
ties understood the reference because all summer long they
had prayed while I battled an intestinal parasite. Yup—it was
as disgusting as you're imagining.

Sometimes I refer to the nasty creature that took up residence in my bowels as Juan, because I think I picked him up in San Miguel de Allende, Mexico, on a captivating writers retreat. The irony was that this courageous move of mine—to take a trip, without my spouse, to join a group of women I didn't know well—helped shape the book you're reading *and* spun me into a deep cycle of depression right before my first book, *No More Holding Back*, launched into the world.

I was F-I-N-E during the trip to San Miguel, perfectly healthy and delightfully happy. According to my doctor, some parasites need time to—wait for it—incubate. *Shivers.* Needless to say, Juan ruined my summer. When I was not running to the bathroom, I was laid up in bed throwing lavish pity parties. While my family traveled without me to the beach, made memories for a lifetime, and Instagrammed to prove it, I was doubled over in pain, slamming my phone into my mattress and turning my fist up to the sky.

I had multiple doctors' visits, a CT scan, and three rounds of antibiotics. A lifetime supply of empty Imodium A-D bottles littered my house because Juan wouldn't leave my body. Forty days later, when we were still unsure of the kind of culprit, my doctor suggested "further testing." Having lost all patience, I rolled my eyes at his suggestion.

"Whatever it takes, Doctor, I am willing to do. Just help me get well, please," I told him.

Doc said to hold my sentiments until I understood what further testing would actually mean.

"Quest Diagnostics has the orders for the tests. Look up

the nearest one on your phone, go there, and pick up your containers for a specimen," he said.

Containers? Specimen? Before I could finish saying, "Whuuuut?" he cut me off by repeating, "Just look up the nearest Quest Diagnostics and take it one step at a time."

Turns out, there's a Quest Diagnostics really close to my house. As I rolled up to the parking lot, I thought it ironic that the Tom Thumb grocery store shared a parking lot with the place where people left their blood, urine, and other samples behind. To my horror, in a few seconds of panic I realized they didn't share a parking lot. Quest Diagnostics was *inside the grocery store*. I am permanently disturbed by this reality, friends. PSA: Don't bring me food from Tom Thumb, ever.

On what happened to be book-launch day, per the doctor's orders, I fulfilled my "duties" and returned the containers to the grocery store, *ahem*, I mean, to Quest Diagnostics. Yes. I scooped my own poop the same day my writing career was official. If the Lord was trying to teach me about staying grounded while my dreams were soaring, we can consider his work here done. Message received.

Inevitably, every time I tell this story, there are at least a few people in the audience whose necks move like bobbleheads throughout the whole retelling. They know exactly where the story is going because of their own gloved firsthand experience. However, you don't need to struggle with diarrhea for more than a month or the depression that follows to understand how crappy life can feel.

Metaphorically speaking, the city of Shechem was where lots of dung had been flung, hit the fan, and stunk up the whole area. Although Shechem may be hard to spell and diffi-cult to picture, it's best described as a place where evil gained such a foothold of power that it eventually reigned. When bad things happen to us or the people we love, the location where the trauma, loss, and heartache took place seems to hang an imaginary warning sign cautioning us to keep out. To the first-century readers of the New Testament, Sychar (or Shechem) was such a place. But it was also the same place Jesus entered to talk with the Samaritan woman at the well.

His presence would have been revolutionary, unexpected, and disorienting. We think Jesus doesn't belong in bad places, but he might be the only person who can handle the broken-ness of his surroundings and the mess we've made of our lives. Maybe that's the message you need to hear right now. Jesus goes *there*, with you, for you. Jesus knocks the Do Not Enter sign off any door to find you, and nothing he finds inside will freak him out. He meets us where we are and redeems every situation with his presence. We are going to look closely at Shechem to understand why Jesus chose this location to speak into the Samaritan woman's life.[1]

Many tragic and traumatic events took place in Sychar (or Shechem) in the Old Testament, one being the rape of Dinah in Genesis 34. If sexual violence toward women is a trigger for you, hear me when I tell you it wasn't your fault. You didn't deserve it. God is not okay with the way you were abused, and you are so loved.

The Bible does not shy away from exposing the disturbing failures of God's people. We may want to look away from our faith history, filled with proof that *all* people fall short of God's holiness, but the Scriptures won't let us overlook our need for God or the pain we all suffer when systems and situations are broken under the weight of sin. Between resurrection and complete redemption, we are living with the truth that hurt people hurt people. And we are trying to find a way to live with grace and truth. Grace, that Jesus comes close to us with his life, bore our scars in his crucifixion, and destroyed our destroyer in his resurrection. And truth, that he will come to judge the unrighteous, defeat sin once and for all, and bring those who love him home.

I can't wait for you to see how Jesus validates our stories, remembers our pain, restores our dignity, and gives us a voice. But first, we will have to face our history. Notice with me the pattern that emerges when Sychar's history is traced under its Old Testament name, Shechem.

SHECHEM WAS A REALLY BAD PLACE

At first, Shechem was a host to God himself. Genesis 12 tells us that Abram built an altar to God in Shechem. This historic setting sounds like a safe place to meet God, worship him, and experience the peace of his presence. That's what makes the next major biblical reference to Shechem so startling. In Genesis 34, Dinah, the daughter of Jacob and Leah, was raped in Shechem by a man named Shechem. At that point it became a corner of the earth where unspeakable violence toward women happened and where silence about sexual violence toward women became the status quo. We will come back to this later.

In the following chapter of Genesis, we see the patriarch Jacob trying to bury his idols in the ground at Shechem. Imagine this pathetic scene: the great leader of our faith, Jacob, attempting to hide physical evidence of sin, as if the dirt could absolve God's people of idol worship. Jacob's beloved son, Joseph, was sold into slavery in Shechem in Genesis 37, so it became a place where family members turned against family members with murderous intentions and where betrayal ended in human trafficking. What was once an area visited by God and marked by his presence became a crime scene for cover-ups, rape, attempted murder, and the slave trade. It only got worse.

While "Burn it down!" is a rally cry for cynics and protestors, it is also the theme of the book of Judges. The whole book is a dumpster fire. By that I mean the imagery of fire shows up in almost every chapter, leading the reader to believe the failed system of unimpressive judges (except for Deborah, the only exceptional judge in Israel's history) really should have all been burned down. I need a whole other book to discuss that, but for our purposes, I want you to see that tucked into the sad history of Israel, under the judges' leadership, is a story about evil King Abimelech. He was so scary. Every time I have to say his name in public, I cower.

Some would say Abimelech was the evilest king mentioned in all of the Scriptures. He tortured people and reigned with reckless abandon to all of his corrupt and destructive impulses. I shudder to think how terrorized we would all be under such cruel leadership. Murdering seventy of his brothers at one time implies he was numb to death. You can find his story, along with the fact that he was coronated in Shechem, in Judges 9. Not only did men like Shechem from Genesis 34 abuse women there, but the town also became a place where fickle followers empowered abusive men to oppress innocent victims. Evil was not just happening in Shechem; it was celebrated with a crown.

The evil king Rehoboam was also coronated in Shechem (1 Kings 12:1). Although his reign was less severe than King Abimelech's, it was disturbing nonetheless and proved Shechem was a place where people didn't learn from their mistakes. The people of Shechem didn't course-correct by choosing morally upright leaders, even when death would likely consume them because of the evil kings ruling over them.

Told ya—Shechem was a really bad place where wicked things happened.

There was no reason for Jesus to have been in Shechem, except for his divine determination to speak with the woman at the well. His entrance into the town would have caused first-century readers to remember its biblical history in the Old Testament. The mention of Sychar (or Shechem) in John 4 leaves readers wondering, *What's the next horrible thing doomed to happen in that godforsaken place?* To our surprise, what we soon learn is the Savior's presence meant all bets were off. Evil was about to be dismantled.

I think Jesus "had" to go there because that's what Jesus does—he enters into our brokenness. The place needed to be redeemed. Maybe you think the hardships or the trauma you've suffered feel like ancient history still haunting your present and hindering your future. Well, I have good news for you: Jesus specializes in redeeming broken places. What he did for Shechem, I know he can do for you.

CHAPEL SERVICES

"I wanted to tell you I love your curls. What products do you use? But really, can we talk about suicide?"

She was a student at Houston Christian High School, where I preach in chapel services each fall. She was doing her best to conceal the real reason she wanted to confide in me, but she ended up disclosing that my message that morning about the book of Ecclesiastes and my father's suicide hit close to home. She had a loved one considering ending their life.

Weeks before, I'd collaborated with the chaplain of the Christian private school to narrow my message, and as this young woman talked with me, I realized the divine hand that had guided that decision. Thanks to the women's Bible study at my church, I'd been noodling around with the book of Ecclesiastes and the profound disillusionment it seemed King Solomon experienced in his life. I've struggled with anxiety and depression for most of my own life, and I find great comfort in his book.

The chapel talk was intended to be about the hope of the gospel in the midst of suicidal depression. The chaplain and I agreed this would be relevant for the students; the suicide rates are higher for their generation than any before them, and rarely do we speak frankly about it.[2] Wise women like the chaplain have the guts to use the chapel services to talk about true-to-life issues facing our teens. Describing the students as "rowdy, bored, and hungry," the chaplain warned me that it might be difficult to hold their attention. Maybe they were just in rare form, maybe having a woman preacher on stage felt like a unicorn was in the room, or maybe it was because the Scriptures leaped off the pages and into their hearts. I'm not sure. But you could have heard a pin drop when I introduced our topic: suicidal depression. Even their posture shifted. Heads lifted and turned straight, both feet fell to the floor, and you could see neighbors nudging friends awake. There was a line of students waiting to pray with me when I got off stage.

A year later, I asked the same chaplain permission to preach about Dinah's sexual assault in Shechem. My email suggested that I believed the trust I'd earned with the students the year before might prepare them to talk about something just as difficult: sexual violence. She agreed and set me loose to use words like *sexual assault, coercion, harassment, #metoo, #churchtoo,* and *rape.* As you can imagine, my second appearance caused some sobering reactions. The young men and women in the room readied themselves for the "curly-headed lady" to say hard things. It felt like all the air in the room was sucked up into a cloud of concern hovering above the anticipation of my words. From the stage it seemed a few students were even holding their breath to see where this was going. I'll tell you what I told them. Dinah's rape is connected to the Samaritan woman at the well because both stories take place in Shechem. Comparing the women and their experiences uncovers the power of Jesus' presence in our Do Not Enter zones.

DINAH AND THE SAMARITAN WOMAN AT THE WELL

Long story short, Leah and Jacob had a daughter named Dinah who went out one day to visit her friends. Somewhere along the way, the prince's son, Shechem, spotted her, stole her, and attacked her. Abusing her was not enough for Shechem. He became obsessed with her and enlisted his father, Hamor, to help him keep her under his power forever as his wife. Or should we say toy?

When Jacob, one of the fathers of our faith, heard his daughter had been "defiled," he kept silent. Dinah's brothers, on the other hand, were furious, enraged by the disgrace. A deal was then struck between Jacob and his sons and Shechem and his dad regarding the fate of the victimized young girl. She would marry Shechem, her rapist, but in turn, Hamor, Shechem, and their people would have to be circumcised. The terms of negotiation were simply a ploy to give Dinah's brothers an advantage as they schemed revenge. Weakened from their surgeries, Hamor and Shechem and their people would be unable to defend themselves from Dinah's brothers. Their plan worked, and Genesis 34 ends with mass murder and more women being brutalized.

Although Jacob seemed unconcerned with Dinah's pain, he reprimanded his sons' behavior with scolding remarks about how their revenge would bring trouble upon himself. Trouble to Jacob? Wow. Never mind Dinah's troubles. Dinah became a discarded widow, and we never hear about her again in the Scriptures except when she's mentioned as one of Leah's daughters (Genesis 46:15).

In Dinah's culture, women were objects to be acquired to produce male heirs for their husbands. The value assigned to a baby girl was woefully less than that of a male child. One way we know this to be true is the lack of daughters listed in the Bible at their birth. Dinah makes biblical history by being one of the very few (Gen. 30:21). And we see in her story that being Israelite "royalty" did not shelter her from oppression. In contrast, the Samaritan woman at the well is nameless in the text. But don't miss the truth that Jesus knew her name. We may not, but he did. While Dinah is the first named daughter in the Bible, and her experience represents evil's accessibility to even the most prestigious, the nameless woman at the well in John 4 represents all women, all Gentiles, and ultimately, all people.

In Dinah's story we were introduced to her father's landlord, Hamor the Hivite, who was the "region's chieftain" (Gen. 34:2), and Hamor's son, Shechem. The saying "like father, like son" rings true for these two. Hamor and Shechem, both princes of terror, sharply contrast the main man in John 4, Jesus, the Prince of Peace. Whereas Hamor and Shechem gave their town a bad name with their intimidation, Jesus, the one who knows all our names, ushers in harmony and safety with his presence.

When Dinah casually ventured out to connect with her friends, the mood was laid back. Just another day in the neighborhood. But while Dinah was minding her own business, Shechem was hunting his prey. We get the sense from the story that we need to hide from his wandering eye and protect ourselves from his looming presence. Compare that to the nameless Samaritan woman at the well who encountered the Prince of Peace. The Samaritan woman was also minding her own business, but when Jesus sat down near the well, his posture spoke to his vulnerability. Our Savior was a safe stranger to approach. Unlike Shechem, Jesus just wanted to talk.

What gets me every time in Dinah's story is her father's silence. Adding insult to injury, Jacob, the man in her life tasked with her protection and provision, seemed uncaring at best. A sober-minded reading of his reaction to his daughter's rape shows him complicit in her trauma and a coconspirator in her demise. Not only do we *not* have a record of him ripping his clothes in mourning, shouting to the rooftops with anger, cursing his daughter's tormentor, or falling to his knees in grief, we have no record of him talking to his daughter about her most painful moment. Shockingly, just a few chapters later, Jacob's reaction to his son Joseph's rumored death is full of emotional expressions we should have seen in Dinah's story too. What kind of godly parent abandons a young girl to process her trauma on her own? Apparently, the same kind of guy willing to sell her off to a man confirmed to be a possessive sexual predator who was admittedly infatuated with his daughter. Why did Jacob sell her out? He bought his land from Shechem's dad, Hamor, the most powerful man in the area. To confront the sin could have meant disrupting the existing power structures and threatening his own power and possessions.

Contrast Jacob's silence to the long conversation Jesus initiated with an unclean woman in Samaria. Even though Jesus knew every part of her story, he wanted *her* to tell it. He listened. He cared. Allowing her own voice to speak her truth, Jesus engaged her in "one of the longest continuous narratives" in the book of John.[3] It's as if Jesus wanted to remind you and me that we are worth a sit-down, face-to-face conversation. Jesus gave the Samaritan woman the dignity Dinah should have received from her father, Jacob. In doing so, Jesus gave away his power. He did not dominate the exchange, disrespect her by "mansplaining" her experience, or fail to believe her. Twice Jesus told her, "What you have said is true," confirming his trust in her testimony and validating her story. Did you know Dinah was never heard in all of the Scriptures? Never. Her perspective was never given a voice. Jesus not only gave the Samaritan woman a voice; he also then gave her an audience to proclaim her truth—and the truth that Jesus is the Savior of the world.

Dinah's story ends in Genesis 34 with genocide, and you can't help but close the chapter disappointed that there was no redemption in the ending. In sharp contrast, the Samaritan woman's story in John 4 ends with many in the town being saved. Dinah's story begins with a dead-end future and ends in the death of a whole people group. The Samaritan woman's story begins with a curious encounter and ends in a whole group of people finding eternal life. While Dinah and the nameless woman at the well are *connected* through Shechem, Jacob and Jesus are *contrasted* through Shechem.

Jacob's failures as a patriarch left a woman vulnerable, but Jesus is better than Jacob in every respect. In fact, this was one of the questions the Samaritan woman asked of Jesus in John 4:12: "You aren't greater than our father Jacob, are you?" The answer is yes. Yes! Jesus *is* greater. She knew the Jewish Messiah shouldn't have been in the Do Not Enter zone that was Samaria, but he came anyway. She got what Dinah deserved: redemption.

I think God is sending us a message about what he can do with our Shechem-like places. No longer will silence about rape be tolerated here. No longer will we tolerate abusive men in positions of power. It ends with Jesus. He enters into our broken places like he owns them—and he redeems them. No place is too broken, no person too far gone for Jesus to change the narrative with his presence.

The question I asked the students of Houston Christian High School is this: If this is what Jesus can do with Shechem, what do you think he can do with your in-between places?

I've never been the victim of sexual violence, but as I reread what took place in Shechem, I'm mindful that Jesus can redeem any horrible situation. He can handle your addictions to porn, one-night stands, sexting, shopping, pills, gaming, cutting, or social media. He can handle a bereaved or angry or insufferable mother. He can handle the hate in our hearts manifested by gossip, slander, and lying. He can handle years of unemployment, confusion about your calling, and stubbornness to follow his lead. He can handle racism, sexism, and classism. And he never suffers compassion fatigue from grieving with you. Never. When everyone else is tired of your prayer requests, complaints, confusion, and heartache, Jesus is not. He comes near.

To the shock of many and the rescue of all, nothing is off-limits to Jesus. So why not embrace his presence in our brokenness? Instead of trying to hide from him, why not throw out our hands and motion for him to see all the mess for what it is and invite him to do what only he can—redeem?

TEST RESULTS

As I made my way into Quest Diagnostics, I was greeted by a nurse who rushed me behind closed doors to help me pick up the doctor's order of supplies. Using tools, visual aids, and hand motions that will haunt me forever, the nurse tried to explain to me the right way to fill the containers. As disgusting as this may be, what she stressed most to me was that the specimen needed to reach the designated line drawn inside the containers. Apparently one cannot get accurate test results without the right amount of poop. Picture me with my eyes shut tight, gripping the seat of my chair while I rocked forward and backward over and over while repeating, "No. You can't be serious. Please no. No."

Nurses are supposed to help us calm down, and yet this one just started giggling at my reactions to her instructions. She tried to encourage me with the fact that lots of people have had to do this. Lady, the fact that multitudes of strangers have had to put their own feces in a container and then bring it into this grocery store, past the food aisles, into this section of Tom Thumb did *not* bring me comfort.

What if our in-between places were like my gut check? Sometimes we're worn down by how much crap, literal and metaphorical, we have to deal with. That's when we need to turn to Jesus to get us through. There's no doubt our spiritual health professional, Jesus, is willing and able to show us what we need to do to find hope, peace, and confidence right where we are. Because if Jesus can redeem Shechem, a really crappy place, he can redeem whatever Shechem represents in your own life.

When our in-between places start to feel like a broken record, it can lead to hopelessness, exhaustion, and disillusionment. Am I reading your mail? Discerning our callings, enjoying our assignments, and embracing our seasons are nearly impossible while fighting off doubts that our situations will never change.

Enter Jesus. He's not done with you yet. Your life *can* be different. Because Jesus is still on his throne, and he is still changing our stories. Equipped with more ways to make peace with our past, the next chapter will help you believe a fresh start is still possible. Yes, even for you.

Discussion Questions

1. If Shechem were a place in your life, where would it be?
2. How does Jesus' presence in Shechem change your perspective of the bad place you are in?
3. Describe a time when Jesus' presence felt most real in your life.
4. What spiritual practices help you experience God's nearness?
5. What about the connection between Dinah and the Samaritan woman stood out to you most?

6. What about the contrast between Jacob and Jesus stood out to you most?

Study Guide

Visit www.katarmstrong.com/theinbetweenplace to download the free study guide. Materials for chapter 2 include

- a list of every mention of Shechem in the Bible
- a chart contrasting Dinah's story with that of the woman at the well

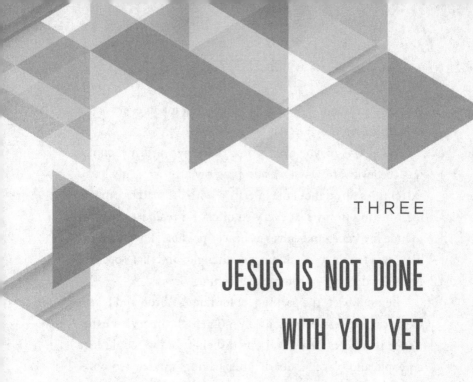

THREE

JESUS IS NOT DONE WITH YOU YET

Where there's hope, there's life. It fills us with
fresh courage and makes us strong again.

—ANNE FRANK

Wearing leather-looking pants to my husband's head-pastor job interview ranks as one of my most embarrassing moments. Pleather on the front, business black on the back—goodness, it was cringeworthy. What possessed me to sport edgy pants for a formal ministry interview is beyond me. I've since donated the evidence of my misjudgment. To all those deeply concerned about the top I wore for the interview, I'd like the record to show that it was an extremely modest, chunky sweater tunic.

You can breathe a sigh of relief; it covered me in every sense of the phrase.

What was maybe even worse than my wardrobe choice was the awkward way I was draping my arms over my lower extremities throughout the interview with the search committee. Shifting in my seat every so often, I'd readjust my arms to hide my knees and calves as best as possible. I bet it looked like I was trying to touch my toes all night, and that's because *I was*. By the way, Aaron rocked the interview.

Before we left the parking lot for home, Aaron and I wept in the car, expressing what a holy moment the interview experience had been for us and our disbelief that we could love a people and place so dearly after having only visited once. Dallas Bible Church was home; Aaron just knew it. I agreed with commensurate optimism and joked that he should thank me for providing him with his first sermon illustration, the rock-'n'-roll pants.

Aaron is one of the best preachers I've ever heard and as pastoral as they come, but Dallas Bible Church's search committee and search firm had been interviewing for months and had already selected their top two candidates for the final stages of hiring a lead pastor when they agreed to interview Aaron. His late entrance into the process didn't inspire hope from my perspective.

By an act of grace, the Lord helped Aaron advance in the process. For our interview with the elder board, the governing authorities of the church, I was dressed appropriately, I assure you. But no fashion choice could have prepared me for Aaron's speech during that final interview. Using chopping motions with his hands to accompany his declaration, he made it clear that this would not be a two-for-one hire. When I heard him make this statement, my neck popped his direction with the same force as a chiropractic adjustment, and my eyelashes practically touched my eyebrows in shock. Concerned everyone in the room could see my heart beating outside my chest, I stared at Aaron while he continued to preach.

"Kat and I have been married for twelve years, and it's taken us a long time to find where she flourishes most. We've worked too hard and too long to see her diminish because of a role I take in ministry. Whatever you decide for Dallas Bible Church as it relates to my role as lead pastor, make sure your decision takes into account my wife's full-time work, busy travel schedule, and calling to preach the Bible outside the walls of any church we join. I will not risk her calling for any job offer. As fiercely as I know possible, I will advocate for and protect her ministry as if it were my own. Upon taking a lead-pastor job, I do not expect her to lessen her commitment to her work unless the Lord makes it clear to *her*. And as the leaders of Dallas Bible Church, you should do the same. Make no assumptions that she will be my sidekick. Kat is my wife, and that is the role we want her to fulfill as it relates to my vocational ministry."

Like an onlooker to a Forrest Gump Ping-Pong match, my head volleyed with glances back and forth from the elders to Aaron. Aaron showed me new dimensions of his love. He took up a mantle I didn't know I needed him to hold. The courage required of him to set realistic expectations and boundaries with the organizational leaders determining his fate was not lost on me. In my estimation, he risked his dream job to ensure my flourishing. If the old saying "Start as you mean to go" is true, Aaron Armstrong intended to start his next season of ministry without any questions about where I stood in the picture.

I share this story with you because I know what it's like to be given the opportunity to start with a clean slate. It's liberating. Truthfully, I've never felt constrained by any church where Aaron has been in leadership, so I wasn't carrying that kind of baggage. But Aaron knew I had concerns about my role as a lead-pastor's wife. What would people expect of me? It wouldn't take long before I would fret about what other pastors' wives did and how. What would most churchgoers assume would be my responsibilities? It only takes one conversation with a burned-out ministry spouse to realize that in some churches, the pastor's wife is saddled with endless demands without warning.

As much as Aaron's job search was an in-between place for him, it was for me too. Actually, I think I'm allergic to the unknown. Throughout our relationship we'd started new jobs and transitioned several times, but this move, unlike any other, began in unison and clarity because everyone involved in the hiring decision was on the same page about both of our roles. The sure footing that followed is something I want you to enjoy too.

You don't need a husband, or a husband like Aaron, to experience the freedom to make a shift in your life. You need Jesus, because he is the origin of fresh starts. I have more to tell you about how Aaron's continued support shaped our new start, but for now I want you to know that his time as a candidate was months of an in-between place for him, which he handled with grace and truth. As usual, I find myself aspiring to be more like Aaron and am grateful his example points me to Jesus, the one who makes new starts possible.

If your in-between spot feels like a scratched record caught on its spinner, looped on the same recurring issue, don't let hopelessness, exhaustion, or disillusionment be the notes stuck on repeat. You can rest assured that whatever *it* may be, *it* won't always be like this. Like a hand from the sky, God can reach down to reset the record spinner and put a new song of peace in our hearts.

The apostle John introduced us to the God of new-song possibilities through his gospel account in the New Testament. Looking at the way John connected the book of Genesis to his own book is like listening to two accomplished musicians collaborate to create new sounds.

GENESIS CREATOR AND BEGINNING MAKER

I'm a self-professed choir nerd. The melodies of a choral ensemble warming up before state competitions are the most memorable soundtracks of my high school years. Show choir, girls' pop, quartet—you name the combination, I wanted to sing in it. Rarely a stand-alone soloist, I was at my best harmonizing with a group. Singing for the choir and leading as an officer created a very tidy category for my identity development. My before- and after-school activities were largely consumed, weekends filled, goals clear, and letterman jacket branded to match my place in my little world.

The older I get, the harder it is to fit into such a neat category. Almost every life change can easily become an existential crisis: *Who am I, really?* We may not know where we belong or how we fit in any given situation, but God does. And we can trust he will be with us wherever we are on our journeys.

God has proven time and time again that he will make a way to be with us, most notably through his Son, Jesus Christ. This person, Jesus, who was fully God and fully man, is the one who brings heaven to earth. While we are looking for launching points into new opportunities or transition markers that confirm we are moving in the right direction, we can be sure that no matter where we are or where we end up, God will make his way there.

If you don't have the energy, hope, or faith to follow Jesus, take heart: he comes to you. Maybe you are working your very first job, restarting school to finish your degree, becoming a first-time mom, or beginning a new life after a major loss. Are these starting points causing you to question your purpose? Remember, God specializes in a genesis of any kind.

"In the beginning" is the phrase both Moses and John chose to open their records of history. Whether it's through Moses' testimony in the book of Genesis about our *first* beginnings—"In the beginning God created the heavens and the earth" (Gen. 1:1)—or John's testimony in his gospel about our *new* beginnings—"In the beginning was the Word, and the Word was with God, and the Word was God" (John 1:1)—one thing is clear: Jesus is the Genesis Creator and Beginning Maker. Three little words, *in the beginning*, show us that when we read our Bibles, we should treat John in the New Testament as a parallel work to Genesis in the Old.

We see this most clearly in John 1 when John teaches us that *the Law* came through Moses and *grace* came through Jesus. The Law wasn't just a set of rules; it was the way God intended people living before the time of Christ to be in a relationship with him. While it can be confusing, the Law's purpose was to connect unholy, God-trusting people to a holy, trustworthy God. Verses later, John would explain that while the Law came through Moses, grace and truth come through Jesus. Revealing a whole new dimension to God's love, Jesus' incarnation, his presence in bodily form, made change possible.

When I doubt my abilities, when I'm fearful about the future, or when I step out in faith, I would much rather discover confidence, peace, and security before moving forward. Instead, I should focus my energy on an awareness of God's grace and truth, which come through Christ and meet me where I am. As we look to find our place in this world, or to move on from a painful situation, may grace and truth mark our path forward.

Never do I need to hear John's description of Jesus more than when my future feels dark. Christ is the Light. He was present and active in the creation of the world. His "light shines in the darkness," and the darkness cannot overcome his presence (John 1:5). In him, we have all received "grace upon grace" (John 1:16).

Maybe you need to hear that your future is bright. Not because of self-help, self-discovery, or a deep dive into the Enneagram personality chart—your future is bright because nothing can darken Jesus' plans for you. This is not to say that suffering is a thing of your past. Suffering and failure are a part of being human. But I know that God's goodness and mercy will follow you all the days of your life (Ps. 23:6).

To those who feel undeserving of a new beginning, remember, it's grace. Grace upon grace, actually. No one deserves it, but it's available to us now through Jesus. Wherever you need "in the beginning" to be a part of your story, God is able to create and re-create.

While the possibility of a fresh start is encouraging in its own right, you and I know it is not enough. We have to find a way to live our day-to-day without a shame cycle weighing us down. Starting over is great if we end up in a new place, but what do we do about second chances that seem to turn into the same ol' story? If history repeats itself, what is there to say we aren't all destined to be perpetually stuck?

Call me simple-minded, but the answer is Jesus. His presence can change the narrative. In the story of the woman at the well, John showed us she was stuck in Samaria, surviving in crappy Shechem and likely expecting things would never change. That is until a Jewish man claiming to be God offered a throwback to a very common story, but with an added plot twist that she never saw coming.

WELL, WELL, WELL

Hallmark Christmas movies have their haters, but none of them live in the Armstrong household. Although we are super disappointed in the lack of diversity in the actors, we love the predictability of each story line; the movies are addictive. Unlike our day jobs in ministry, we can stare at that screen and watch a story wrap up with a beautiful red-velvet bow and a kiss in ninety minutes. Yes, we know there is a scene template for each movie; we don't care. We don't just accept the trite conclusions; we celebrate them. No prolonged hardships, unanswered prayers, or unfinished business. Each happy ending makes us smile.

If only reality played out the same way. I would guess that you feel as though your life has a familiar story line, too, but it doesn't always end up like a Hallmark Christmas movie. Whether you're stuck in a sin cycle, shame cycle, or relationship cycle, you feel like a hamster on a wheel. The woman at the well could relate, and so can I. I imagine one of our Enemy's favorite phrases to speak over us is *"Well, well, well, look what we have here,"* as if to remind us that a new way of living is as likely as a Hallmark movie being true to life. But discouragement is a liar. It won't always be the way it has been. Change really *is* possible. That's because Jesus is the Genesis Creator, a Beginning Maker, and our powerful Change Agent.

Although distance and time separate us from the events in the Old Testament, to a first-century New Testament disciple, everything in the Old connected to the New. For instance, it wouldn't take long before an early Christ follower heard about Jesus' conversation with the woman at the well and started to think of the three "betrothal-type scenes" detailed throughout Scripture that also happen to have taken place at a well.[1] Rebekah's, Rachel's, and Zipporah's engagement stories have similar elements. Each story includes a bridegroom or his servant traveling to a foreign place to secure a bride close to a well.[2] It was as familiar a story line to the first-century disciples as a Hallmark Christmas movie plot is to Team Armstrong. As soon as the unmarried Samaritan woman approached the well in Shechem, the audience would have been predicting how the story would end badly. Except this time, Jesus was the plot twist. As I mentioned before, the book of Genesis and the book of John are parallel works, and Moses and John, the authors of those books, are connected too. I marvel that three of the four betrothal scenes are either in the book of Genesis or about Moses, and the fourth of four engagement stories is in the book of John.

REBEKAH

In the first of four scenes at the well (Gen. 24:10–30), the bridegroom was Isaac, whose father, Abraham, sent a servant to Samaria to find a wife for his son. The servant prayed that God would show him the woman who was supposed to be Isaac's wife. Rebekah was coming to a well to draw water when he arrived. The servant spoke with Rebekah, asking her for a drink of water. When she offered her water not only to him but to his camels, he knew she was the one. Rebekah was the woman at the well drawing water, and eventually Isaac and Rebekah married. Rebekah's story is similar to that of the Samaritan woman in John 4 in that she was an unmarried woman, drawing water at a well, approached about a drink, and asked a few questions. Probably the difference that stands out most to me is Rebekah was a virgin, and the woman at the well in John 4 most certainly was not. I think Jesus intended to undo and remake what it meant to be a daughter of Samaria, an unwed woman, dependent upon others for survival. And I think he did so by repurposing a pattern and giving it a Jesus ending.

RACHEL

In Genesis 29:1–12, the bridegroom was Jacob, who went to Samaria to find a wife and ended up meeting a woman named Rachel at a well. After a lot of drama with his future father-in-law, Jacob married two sisters, Rachel *and* Leah. Jacob fell in love with Rachel at the well while watering her sheep, but her deceitful father, Laban, tricked Jacob into working for Rachel's hand. And then on their wedding night, Laban gave Jacob his oldest daughter, Leah, instead. Can you imagine? Jacob was livid. And it's obvious Laban had been conspiring for years to pull off the trick.

This story didn't have a happy ending. The sisters competed with each other's fertility for years. The power struggle, manipulation, and shame between the two women and their slaves rival any modern-day soap opera. Leah needed to bear Jacob's children to earn his attention because his true and first love was Rachel. Rachel needed to bear Jacob's children to earn her honor because their culture elevated procreation as a woman's only purpose in life.

ZIPPORAH

In Exodus 2:15–21, Moses was the bridegroom. He sat down next to a well in Midian before meeting his wife Zipporah.

The Bible gives us fewer details about this betrothal scene, but several key elements are connected to our story of interest in John's gospel. Namely, Moses came to Zipporah's rescue at the well and ensured that she and her sisters would be able to get the water they needed. Hundreds of years later, Jesus would sit next to the well in Shechem and come to the Samaritan woman's rescue. But not through the water of the well. Instead, her rescue would be through the "living water," God's presence in her life.

THE SAMARITAN WOMAN

By the time they got to the Samaritan woman at the well in John 4, first-century disciples would have sensed the familiarity in the story like a Hallmark Christmas movie. Many times they had heard about women at wells approached by men traveling into their area from a distant land to secure a wife. The woman at the well might have assumed, too, that Jesus' intention was to propose. But Jesus is greater than Jacob, remember? The Savior did not need a wife; he was looking for disciples.

Jesus, like Abraham's servant in Genesis 24, was God's representative on earth to "distribute his master's riches and inheritance."[3] Jesus was like Jacob in that he arrived at the well in the middle of the day, and he was like Moses in that he sat down next to the well and was not recognized. But unlike Abraham, Jacob, or Moses, Jesus created a plot twist by teaching on the "living water," something we will talk more about very soon. Point being, just when you think the shame narrator of your story is about to say, *Well, well, well, what do we have here?* Jesus shows up and proves with his presence that your story has a Jesus ending.

My own shame narrator lies to me with statements like *Your worst-case scenario is inevitable. You're destined to failure. It's not going to work out. This is probably a lost cause. You deserve this outcome.* I'm not proud to share those direct quotes plucked from my cluttered brain. Letting you into those lies in my head feels like I'm wearing half-pleather pants again, awkward and insecure. And I'm not even a pessimist, y'all. I'm a let's-do-this, why-not-try, I-have-a-big-dream kind of gal. But I've got a record spinning in my head just like you do, because of habit and fear.

As Christians, we know that fear and lies are evidence the Enemy is messing with us, distracting us from our purpose. Brené Brown gives our struggle a name: foreboding joy. In her book *Daring Greatly*, she describes how practiced most of us are at resisting joyful feelings to protect ourselves from disappointment.[4] What would your mental tapes reveal? Do you wait for the other shoe to drop? Are you flow-charting all the worst-case scenarios and how you would deal with each tragedy? That, my friends, is the loss of hope. We are so practiced at living disappointed, we have to retrain our hearts and minds to dare to hope. Hope in your thought life could sound like this:

- What God starts, he brings to completion (Phil. 1:6).
- All good things come from God (James 1:17).

- God is able, always (Eph. 3:20).
- God will make a way (Isa. 43:19).
- Goodness and faithful love will follow me all the days of my life (Ps. 23:6).
- God is my friend (John 15:15).
- God has good plans for me. I can trust his plan (Rom. 8:28).
- God will be with me every step of the way (Isa. 43:2).
- God never tires (Isa. 40:28).

If you are at the end of your rope, wishing for it all to be over, stay with me. Your broken record of a life is just one encounter with Jesus away from redemption, restoration, and wholeness.

It might feel safe to assume that the woman at the well in Shechem would experience something like Rebekah, Rachel, or Zipporah, but Jesus' conversation didn't lead to a proposal. Jesus led the woman at the well, and leads *us*, to a whole new way of living and the self-sustaining presence called the "living water." Living in the in-between is difficult, but hope is not lost. Doomed is not how your story ends. Because *at his word* our past has no power over our future. Because *in his presence* we have everything we could ever need.

If we embodied these truths, really internalized them as our own, our resilience factor would skyrocket. With every disappointment, we'd respond with life-giving truths that speak of our bright future. We would feel the hard parts of being on the down-and-out, but we would shake ourselves off and determine to keep going. We would look to the ends of our stories and hold on for hope.

We can find that end-of-story hope in the gospel of John, one of the apostle's five books that he contributed to the New Testament, and where we are spending most of our time. He also wrote 1 John, 2 John, 3 John, and Revelation. He was probably very young when he wrote his gospel account and retold the story of the woman at the well in Shechem. But as an old man, he penned Revelation, an apocalyptic vision of the way the world as we know it will end and the new heaven and new earth will begin.

The imagery John used in his gospel shows up all over his last and final book, the words that end the Christian Scriptures. One theme that carries through is the "water of life." God said he is the "Alpha and the Omega, the beginning and the end," and that he will "freely give to the thirsty from the spring of the water of life" (Rev. 21:6). It is as if God knows that any conversation you and I have with him about the "beginning and the end" has to center on his character and his sustaining presence in our lives. That's why the next section of this book, which is about finding hope in your present, will add new dimensions to John 4:6–18 and the dialogue between Jesus and the woman at the well.

THE START OF SOMETHING GOOD

The last and final step in Aaron's hiring process was preaching on a Sunday morning, followed by a congregational vote to affirm the elders' choice. Aaron's sermon was straight fire. The passion pouring out of his soul could only be described as humble devotion. He communicated his dedication to the people of Dallas Bible Church and his commitment to seeing all those in his care flourish. In the same way Aaron helped shape my new start during his interview process, he continues to serve his church: advocating for others with grace and truth.

In between the time he was affirmed in April and his start date in June, our family started attending the church's services and visiting small groups and Sunday school classes. On one visit to a Sunday school class, all the attendees went around the room to introduce themselves. We couldn't get over the kindness of DBC members. They are well practiced in love, and we are learning from their example on a regular basis. When it came our turn, everyone, including me, turned our eyes to Aaron so he could introduce us. He did something I didn't see coming. He announced to the class that they would have lots of opportunities to get to know him over the years, so he wanted me to take the remainder of the class time and share about Polished. Aaron looked at me and said, "Go ahead, babe."

That is the way he leads. He invites others to go ahead of him. Aaron's not perfect; I don't have to explain that to you. And the point of these stories is not his leadership style. The message I want you to take away is that if Aaron's actions created freedom for me and the members of his church, how much more can the actions of the Genesis Creator, Beginning Maker, and Change Agent re-create your in-between places? Could he shut up the shame narrator in your head? Yes. Could his plot twists release you from a hopeless situation? Yes. Absolutely, yes. Jesus is not done with you yet.

Discussion Questions

1. If you have a shame narrator, what does it say to you?
2. In what area of your life would you like to experience change or break a pattern?
3. If you successfully implemented change, how would your life be better?
4. What would a "Jesus ending" look like in your season of life?
5. In what ways does Jesus' presence in your story enable you to change?
6. What is the most significant change you have experienced in life so far?

Study Guide

Visit www.katarmstrong.com/theinbetweenplace to download the free study guide. Materials for chapter 3 include

- an article about the betrothal scenes in the Bible
- the Hope Prayer Guide

PART 1 SUMMARY

Together we've zeroed in on John 4:1–6, taking with us three crucial truths about making peace with our past.

1. Each step of your journey has purpose. Just like Jesus' travels from Judea to Galilee with a stop in Samaria, the most in-between place of all places, every step on our path forward is an opportunity to encounter Jesus.
2. Even crappy places can be redeemed. Like Jesus' stop in Shechem, a really crappy place, the most painful parts of our own lives can be healed with Jesus' presence. Some of our most hope-filled conversations with God happen in the dark nights of our souls.
3. Jesus is not done with you yet. The same God "in the beginning" of Genesis is the "in the beginning" of John's gospel. Making something from nothing is his superpower. Change in any story pattern in your life is possible in Jesus.

PART TWO

FIND HOPE IN YOUR PRESENT

Jacob's well was there, and Jesus, tired out by his journey, was sitting by the well. It was about noon.

A Samaritan woman came to draw water, and Jesus said to her, "Give me a drink." (His disciples had gone to the city to buy food.) The Samaritan woman said to him, "How is it that you, a Jew, ask a drink of me, a woman of Samaria?" (Jews do not share things in common with Samaritans.) Jesus answered her, "If you knew the gift of God, and who it is that is saying to you, 'Give me a drink,' you would have asked him, and he would have given you living water." The woman said to him, "Sir, you have no bucket, and the well is deep. Where do you get that living water? Are you greater than our ancestor Jacob, who gave us the well, and with his sons and his flocks drank from it?" Jesus said to her, "Everyone who drinks of this water will be thirsty again, but those who drink of the water that I will give them will never be thirsty. The water that I will give will become in them a spring of water gushing up to eternal life." The woman said to him, "Sir, give me this water, so that I may never be thirsty or have to keep coming here to draw water."

Jesus said to her, "Go, call your husband, and come back." The woman answered him, "I have no husband." Jesus said to her, "You are right in saying, 'I have no husband'; for you have had five husbands, and the one you have now is not your husband. What you have said is true!"

—JOHN 4:6–18 NRSV

FOUR

FIND SAFE PEOPLE TO SHARE YOUR STORY WITH

When someone shows you who they
are, believe them the first time.

—MAYA ANGELOU

At one time I would have boasted to you that I have gut feelings about a person's character, and those assessments are usually right. This time my Spidey sense was wrong. Turns out, what I considered to be normal friendship friction was actually falsehood.

One night a wave of suspicion crashed over me as I was processing with Aaron what I considered to be friend drama. As the waves flooded my thoughts, it occurred to me that maybe something deeper was going on. I believe that premonition was the Holy Spirit showing me something I didn't want to see about one of my friends. Since I've yet to meet someone unsplashed by tears when a friendship unravels, I know you understand my pain.

Robert De Niro's character in *Meet the Fockers* perfectly describes the suspicion we may feel as he hesitantly gives Greg, the man asking for his daughter's hand in marriage, the imagery of a "circle of trust."[1] As a protective father and former intelligence officer, Robert's character, Jack, almost sabotages his daughter's happiness to satisfy his skepticism. Jack puts Greg through the wringer, even resorting to a lie detector test. Like Jack, when we are trying to discern who should be in and out of our own circle of trust, we can be overly cautious. If we are not careful, we risk letting the wrong people into our circle of trust. If we are *too* careful, we risk keeping the right people out. Jack wants to protect his daughter and insulate his family, but his suspicion causes him to test Greg's intentions in spite of all the evidence that he is a good man worthy of his daughter. The comedy helps us accept that Jack represents anyone who has trouble trusting others. I see myself in Jack. Maybe you do too.

Barna Research Group partnered with humanitarian organization World Vision on the Connected Generation project to study loneliness among young people ages eighteen to thirty-five across twenty-five countries and nine languages. The study of 15,369 survey respondents concluded that "despite being a hyper-connected and globally minded generation, many young adults say they feel lonely.

Fifty-seven percent . . . sense a connection to people around the world, but just one in three . . . says they feel deeply cared for by those around them."[2] I don't think this is just a young-person issue. We can have a bazillion friends on any social platform with a robust social calendar but feel totally isolated from deep and meaningful relationships. Almost anyone can know about you through your online profiles, but who actually knows you? You might have tons of views on your posts, but who knows the backstory to your Instagram stories? Who sees you behind the filters and hashtags?

Finding and cultivating adult friendship is like shaving your knees. For true connection, you can't just glide through relationships unintentionally. It's a tricky business, discerning how close you need to be with a new friend before you bare it all around an area of your life that is tender. Going deep fast can create intimacy, but if we're not careful, even the smallest nick to our feelings can make us flinch from meaningful connections altogether. Who among us hasn't sworn off shaving around our knee bend and determined to only wear pants for the rest of our lives when we accidentally cut ourselves? Who hasn't asked, *Who will be trustworthy with my story? Who will love me in spite of my shortcomings? Whom can I really count on when life is challenging?* These are the kinds of questions we often rehearse before we become vulnerable with someone about our true selves.

It only takes one deep wound from a friend or family member before we start to guard ourselves from being hurt again. Whether it's a child abandoned or neglected by a parent, a sibling rivalry that ends on nonspeaking terms, a cruel and public breakup, the silent killer of "ghosting," or infidelity of an intimate partner, the cuts we bear can't be healed with a simple Band-Aid. It takes soul work, trust, and long-suffering vulnerability to enjoy ride-or-die friendships. We also have to get better at finding *safe* people and trusting them with our stories.

One of my favorite authors, David G. Benner, put it this way in his book *Sacred Companions: The Gift of Spiritual Friendship and Direction*: "Our souls ache for a place of deep encounter with others. Our fears may partially mask this ache, but it won't go away. We want companions for the journey, companions with whom we can share our soul and our journey." Brenner defines a "soul friend" as someone to whom you can bring your whole self.[3] I don't know about you, but that sounds refreshing.

As we wrestle with our in-between place, we've learned that making peace with our past means accepting that we feel stuck, and we might even go so far as to say it's a crappy place that needs to be redeemed. We've seen how Jesus is not done with us yet; he's remaking our lives into stories with Jesus endings.

Now it's time to find hope in our present.

One of the most important ways Jesus is going to change our stories is through our *soul friends*. Digging deeper into John 4, I found Jesus modeled soul friendship to the Samaritan woman at the well—a practice we all need to better understand and internalize. While we read together the private conversation between Jesus and the woman at the well, I think you will see a lesson in learning to entrust our stories to our Savior. But also how to discern whom to bring into our inner circle.

In John 4:6–18, three of Jesus' qualities are revealed: Jesus is approachable, he is a good listener, and he is a truth teller. When no one else can be trusted, when our friends fail us, when our spouses betray us, Jesus is holding space—sacred space—for us to share our stories with him. Since Jesus already knows everything about you, it might be difficult to see the value in sharing your story with him. But as we will see through the woman at the well's encounter with Christ, he wants to hear from you because he loves you.

JESUS IS APPROACHABLE

Tired and weary from his travels, Jesus sat down at the well (John 4:6) in Shechem, positioned to receive the Samaritan woman. Jesus' posture speaks of his humility and the limitations he surrendered to in bodily form. That makes me love him all the more. The Light of the World stooped down to be at an approachable level. It's no secret: pride is a relationship killer. And here we have the Ruler of the world, its Creator, the King of kings and Lord of lords, bending a knee and creating a humble atmosphere for a meaningful relationship. This scene also speaks to his divine intention to have a conversation with the Samaritan woman, a conversation long enough and important enough to require sitting down. How many conversations in my life have started with "Why don't you have a seat?" or "Let's meet face-to-face to talk"? We're living in a day and age when we feel comfortable blasting people with a tweet, breaking up with someone via text, or ghosting someone altogether. But Jesus proved that conveying the value he assigns to women in in-between places requires a face-to-face, sit-down conversation.

Amy Cuddy, a social psychologist at Harvard Business School, gave a famous TED Talk about body language. She suggested getting up out of your chair in the office and striking a Superman pose to boost your confidence before a job interview or uncrossing your arms in a business meeting to signal to your colleagues that you are open to new ideas, all because, as Amy convincingly asserted, "Our nonverbals govern how we think and feel about ourselves." According to Cuddy, our body language and the body language of others are the "lowest tech life hack" available.[4] If pressing our fists into our hips in a wide stance can change our brains and increase our confidence level, imagine the impact of Jesus' choice not to stand when the Samaritan woman arrived. Think what Jesus' posture communicated to her as she approached him—a stranger. To me it speaks to his accessibility and approachability.

All of us have witnessed someone's arms folding in a disagreement, a hair flip to catch someone's attention, or a toddler turning his back on you. In vivid colors, I can relive the moment Aaron dropped on one knee to propose, the wide-eyed grin he shot across a room to signal he had spotted a celebrity, or when his hand squeezed mine after my father passed. Our body language speaks our truth. I wonder if Jesus was sitting the whole time or if he eventually stood up while he was talking with the woman at the well. (Let's ask the Samaritan woman when we meet her.) I'm guessing he was seated the whole time because he was seated for the whole Sermon on the Mount (Matt. 5:1), and sitting down is the first thing he did when he ascended into heaven after his resurrection (Mark 16:19). Imagine the joy that might have filled the Samaritan woman's heart if she learned about Jesus delivering the Sermon on the Mount, a message about the blessings to the poor in spirit, the mourning, the humble, and the thirsty, from the same position in which he proved those points to be true to her. *Mind blown.* Jesus is more approachable than we dare imagine.

According to the author of Hebrews, Jesus is the "radiance of God's glory and the exact expression of [God's] nature, sustaining all things by his powerful word. After making purification for sins, he sat down at the right hand of the Majesty on high" (1:3). Jesus, the one "far above every ruler and authority, power and dominion, and every title given, not only in this age but also in the one to come" (Eph. 1:21), is seated, right now, at the right hand of the Father. He towers over the world, his creation. He rules with unrivaled power and authority, and yet he humbles himself to be in our presence. He is no stranger to bending low to wash feet. If we are looking for safe people, Jesus is the prototype. He "emptied himself by assuming the form of a servant, taking on the likeness of humanity. And when he had come as a man, he humbled himself by becoming obedient to the point of death—even to death on a cross" (Phil. 2:7–8). Jesus bridges the gap between a holy God and an unholy people, like you and me, so we, through our faith in Jesus' life, death, and resurrection, can be in relationship with him.

JESUS IS A GOOD LISTENER

Jack Zenger and Joseph Folkman coauthored an article titled "What Great Listeners Actually Do" for *Harvard Business Review*, which I have reread several times. They grouped their findings into four main points about good listeners:

1. The best listeners don't just remain silent when someone else talks; they "periodically ask questions that promote discovery and insight."
2. Good listeners make other people feel "supported and conveyed confidence in them" so as to create a "safe environment" where differences can be discussed.
3. Good listeners intend to help the person they are listening to, not just win an argument.
4. Good listeners make suggestions that others are able to receive because of the trust built through the conversation.[5]

You know where I'm going with this. Jesus modeled for us all four of these points with tender skill while he listened to the woman's point of view.

He asked the woman at the well for a drink (John 4:7), which is another way of saying, "I want to spend time getting to know you." Twice Jesus affirmed her by saying, "You have correctly said" and "What you have said is true" (vv. 17–18). Jesus believed her, and I bet she felt seen and heard in a world that didn't value her existence, let alone her story. When Jesus presented new theological truths to her, he did so for her good, not to mansplain his views. And he concluded his conversation by telling her to believe that he was Messiah. The best part is, she believed him!

As we saw in chapter 2, Dinah, from Genesis 34, never got an audience with her father, Jacob, to testify about her rape in Shechem. And Jacob is not recorded as ever asking her about her trauma. Instead, her father, in cowardice, allowed his sons to do all the negotiating for Dinah's proposed marriage to her rapist. We also saw that she never got to tell her story, and that her voice is never heard in the Scriptures—only silence. Dinah's word count is zero. But Jesus had one of the longest recorded conversations in the New Testament with the woman at the well. Jesus truly led in a better way, proving he really is better than our faith fathers. As we saw earlier, Jesus already knew the woman's past, but he wanted her to tell her story in her own words from her point of view. Where Dinah was given no voice, Jesus gave it to the woman at the well. In a way only Jesus can, he created an epic redo for both Dinah and the Samaritan woman—and, I think, all women, all Christians, everywhere. Whether our battle is the silence of our leaders or online noise, we are all worth a hard conversation, and he cares to hear from us all.

I've witnessed too many occasions where a Christian resorts to online shaming, passive-aggressive social posts, gossip, or worse, a refusal to meet and talk through issues. I'm guilty of this too. But we can do better. The good news is that God has the emotional bandwidth to hear the contents of our hearts and the scripts in our brains. Thank goodness his compassions won't ever fail us. Plus, we can emulate Jesus, by the power of the Holy Spirit, and have hard conversations too.

If Jesus were sitting right in front of you, what would you want to tell him about your story? I want to encourage you to use the margins in this book or a journal to write out word for word what you would say to him. What could you tell him that you've told no one else? As I think about my own story, my lip starts to quiver and my eyes flood. I tell Jesus often that I miss my dad, and missing him is so complicated because our relationship was complex.

One of my great comforts is knowing I don't have to explain myself to Jesus. He gets me, because he created me and has been present every moment of my life. But I get to express my whole self to him in a way that I may not with my nearest and dearest. Jesus can be our closest companion, our most trusted adviser, and our best soul friend. As in any other relationship, spending time and talking with him are key to building trust and intimacy. Why not entrust more of yourself to the one person who will always accept you for exactly who you are? Although none of our friends will be perfect like Jesus, practicing friendship in relationship with Jesus prepares us to be better friends and to find safe people to share our stories with. Finding peace in your present situation will require as much.

JESUS IS A TRUTH TELLER

Have you ever told a friend, "Thank you for telling me the truth"? Me too. On multiple occasions I can remember thanking my most treasured friends for truth telling. Their honesty has saved me heartaches and headaches. My college bestie, Lori, used to ask me to say this out loud along with her: "Kat, you don't have to decide right now." Lori has had to talk me off several decision cliffs and remind me that one more night of sleep would be a much better option than a hasty jump. My sister-in-law, Lee, comforted me during the early stages of building a nonprofit ministry with the words, "Rest. You've done all that you can do." She knows I'll run myself right into the ground if I am not reminded to chill out. My friend Tiffany sends me the most beautiful handwritten cards, enough to fill a file folder in my desk drawer. She tells me truths about myself and my work that keep me from being too hard on myself. I know that names and faces are popping into your head of the friends who make you feel the most loved. Gracious, truthful friends are the companions we need most in our in-between places.

The West Wing, my favorite TV series, was a show about a noble president and the faithful public servants who supported his vision for a better America. I'm not embarrassed to admit I've seen the series three times all the way through, and almost every single night I like to watch one episode before falling asleep. My most-watched episode includes a scene between Sam Seaborn, who is running for Congress, and one of his closest friends, Toby Ziegler. Sam's campaign is doomed, and everyone knows it but him. That prompts Toby to temporarily resign his post at the White House to help Sam on the campaign trail until the end of the race. The writing is on the wall; Sam is going to lose.

One night after a defeating campaign stop, Sam and Toby

sit down at a bar for a drink, and Toby tells Sam the truth. When Sam asks if he is going to lose, Toby says, "Yeah." When Sam asks if there is any chance of a miracle, Toby says a definitive no. What doesn't make sense to Sam is why Toby left the White House on this fool's errand if the outcome was fated. So he asks Toby why he joined him on the last leg of the trail. Toby says, "You're gonna lose, and you're gonna lose huge. They're gonna throw rocks at you next week, and I wanted to be standing next to you when they did."[6] Sam's so distracted by the impending loss, he responds with sarcasm until Toby convinces him that's *really* the reason he's there. Toby wanted to tell Sam the truth, and he wanted to be with him in his hardest moments. Talk about soul friends.

In John 4:13–14, Jesus said to the woman at the well, "Everyone who drinks of this water will be thirsty again, but those who drink of the water that I will give them will never be thirsty. The water that I will give will become in them a spring of water gushing up to eternal life" (NRSV). Jesus knew her deepest need and met it with theological truth. She was thirsty, not for water but for God's presence in her life, the longing under all of her other longings. Parched for truth and craving security, she didn't need another man in her life; she needed Jesus, the one who meets all our needs. By telling her that everyone who drank from Jacob's well would get thirsty again, he was communicating that the way she was meeting her physical needs wouldn't be enough to meet her spiritual needs. There's no confusing where the living water comes from—only Jesus.

Then Jesus went on to tell the woman her own story of

being married five times and living with someone who was not her husband. Notice with me the sobering teachings Jesus offered to this Samaritan woman. She found hope, the ultimate hope, in words she may not have wanted to hear. And, as we'll see later, she received them with humility.

SAFE PEOPLE

According to psychologists and relationship experts Henry Cloud and John Townsend, authors of *Safe People: How to Find Relationships That Are Good for You and Avoid Those That Aren't*, a safe relationship "draws us closer to God," "draws us closer to others," and "helps us become the real person God made us to be."[7]

As I take inventory of the safe people in my life, one memory comes to mind. One Sunday morning I wanted to encourage my friends Annie and her husband, Pat, who receive churchgoers in between services in the prayer room. I parked in a different spot and walked in through a different entrance, all for the purpose of telling the Mooneys thank you. I wanted them to know so many were being set free through their prayer ministry. Their devotion deserved a high five. I thought I was going into the prayer room to recognize key leaders in our church, but instead Annie recognized in me a need for prayer.

Subconsciously I was carrying a weight of confusion and doubt. I'd just signed with my publisher to write two books, which felt so daunting, especially since I knew what the Lord wanted me to write about in the first one. God was nudging me to share part of my story of experiencing misogyny in seminary and the ways it wounded me. By every measure, I was cleared to entrust this part of myself with the readers of *No More Holding Back*. I felt like I was at the starting line for a marathon, and Jesus was waving the flag to run with the message, but my feet wouldn't move. They were cemented.

Annie welcomed me into the prayer room and wasn't at all surprised to see me, because her spiritual discernment spikes over the Richter scale. I breezed through the room and plopped onto the couch to announce my visit: I was there to encourage them and thank them for their faithful service to Jesus through Dallas Bible Church. They looked at each other like, *Sure, yeah, about that.* Annie described that she had a word pictured in her brain that morning and sensed the Holy Spirit was encouraging her to ask me about the word. I joked with her that I am not a good speller. Humor wouldn't distract Annie; she wrote down the word and then held up a note in her Bible to show me the word there: *ezer.* She said, "Do you know what this word means?" She'd never heard of it before, but she kept seeing those letters together in her brain, and she sensed I was the person to help her understand the meaning.

Good thing both Annie and her husband were present. We needed all six of our hands to scoop my jaw off the ground and back onto my mouth. Stunned, I reached into my purse to pull out my key chain to point at the word engraved upon it: *ezer.*

"You mean this word, Annie?" I said. "*Ezer* is basically

my most favorite word in the whole Bible! It's Hebrew for 'helper.' It's used twenty-one times in the Old Testament, sixteen of those times to describe God himself fighting a battle on our behalf. Some scholars think the word could be better translated 'warrior helper.' It's the word used in Genesis to describe the creation of Eve as Adam's helper. For me, the word *ezer* represents the faith legacy all women carry with them as strong, capable warriors for Christ. Annie! I'm going to devote a whole chapter in my book to this word!"

She couldn't stop bouncing her head in confirmation.

"I knew you were the person to ask, Kat," she said. "I think you are here this morning to receive freedom from something through inner-healing prayer. Something to do with this word, *ezer*. Could Pat and I pray with you?"

It was as though they had gently turned the nozzle on a faucet. My tears started pouring out. Stammering through my emotions, I tried to articulate that the pressure of writing a book was getting to me, and I needed to write about a situation from my past with grace and truth. Guided by the Holy Spirit, Annie and Pat led me through something they call a "Freedom Prayer." Together, we journeyed into my memories of being yelled at in a seminary class and how that experience had the potential to keep me from loving God with all that I am—my heart, soul, mind, and strength. When a fellow student pointed his finger at me and raised his voice to threaten me with the phrase "Just stop!" my *ezer*-ness felt extinguished. I would need all my strength to share this part of my story in the book.

I'll never forget what Annie and Pat emphasized to me

during our prayer time. They said that in Jesus I was safe. I knew it, but I needed to hear it. I was safe. Imagining Christ in that seminary class with me wrecked me. Without knowing it, Annie helped me see Jesus' friendship in my own story. Jesus is accessible and accessible to me. He had been right there with me in one of my troubling in-between seasons of life. Jesus had listened to everything that was said to me all those years ago in that seminary classroom. He could hear all my internal dialogue, and he was privy to every spoken and unspoken part of the conversation. In my mind I was picturing a pink highlighter brushing across Jesus' words to his disciples in the Great Commission: "I am with you always, to the end of the age" (Matt. 28:20). This truth from the Scriptures seemed to melt the cement I had pictured around my feet at the starting line.

Maybe finding safe people means looking for the kind of people who lead us to the one who is always safe: Jesus. What I know for sure is that sharing my story with these two trustworthy people, Annie and Pat, led me to tell Jesus how that classroom experience had impacted me. I knew he was aware, but something in me transformed as I shared with Annie and Pat, and Jesus, from my point of view.

It reminds me of the woman at the well and the liberation she must have felt with Jesus. Annie and Pat are approachable, good listeners who tell the truth because they are modeling their ministry based on Jesus. The confusion and doubt that had felt like concrete boots evaporated in hope when I was able to open up and share.

Writing a book is a significant in-between place for me. The message can be so clear, but getting it on paper and working through the collaboration and editing process can sometimes feel like being in Shechem. Thankfully, I found a source of Christ-centered hope through friends like Annie and Pat.

Jesus changed my story through soul friends, which became a foundation for participating fully in God's mission. You see, God is on a mission to share his love with everyone, and as crazy as it sounds, he's included you and me in his work to see everyone flourish. What we will see together in the next chapter is the radical inclusivity of Jesus. Now that you have the hope of companions in your in-between places, it's time to talk about why some of us feel so left out.

Discussion Questions

1. What is it about Jesus that makes him approachable to you?
2. What are the most important qualities you look for in a trusted friend?
3. Describe a time when a friend disappointed you.
4. If Jesus were sitting in front of you, what would you want to tell him about your story? Why?
5. If Jesus were sitting in front of you, what questions do you think he would ask you?
6. If Jesus were sitting in front of you, what truth do you think he would tell you?

Study Guide

Visit www.katarmstrong.com/theinbetweenplace to download the free study guide. Materials for chapter 4 include

- a link to Amy Cuddy's TED Talk
- a link to the *Harvard Business Review* article
- journal space to tell Jesus your story

FIVE

EMBRACE BELONGING

God calls us *to belong* to the One
who created us and to cultivate that
belonging-ness with all of our hearts.

—RUTH HALEY BARTON

Due to a convergence of my own insecurities and some misogynistic Bible teachings I'd inherited along the way, I used to believe that loving God with our hearts and souls was women's work, and loving God with our minds and strength was men's work. I know. Every time I say it out loud, I want to slap the palm of my hand on my forehead. What was I thinking?

The Bible tells a different story entirely. Both men and women are called by God to love him with all their hearts, souls, minds, and strength, per the Great Commandment (Mark 12:29–30). But I'd been gendering the Great Commandment to fit a worldview that diminished women as second-class contributors in God's kingdom.

As long as I can remember, I've struggled to feel like I belong to God and to his people. Although my struggle has not kept me from growing in my faith or serving his church, the internal arguments I have with myself about my place in this world are a major distraction. If the Bible is correct, and we are all made in God's image to flourish and to work toward the common good of all people, we don't have time to waste wondering if what God says about us is true. We've got to embrace belonging at face value and get on with God's work. Easier said than done, though, especially when we are in an in-between place. When I am in the middle of a work transition or major life change, my inner critic starts shouting so loud that it's hard to concentrate on loving God and loving others.

Almost every week I have the privilege of teaching God's Word. It's my favorite thing to do. While most of those opportunities are with adults, occasionally God opens a door for me to speak to youth, and I love it! God is in the business of using young people to change the world. Some of the standouts that come to mind are the young shepherd David, slaying the giant everyone feared; young queen Esther, risking her life to save her people; the young prophet Jeremiah, delivering pronouncements of doom to the Israelites; and young Mary of Nazareth, receiving with great faith the angel's news of her pregnancy with baby Jesus. In part, I love teaching God's Word to teenagers because looking into their faces as we explore the Scriptures together, I only see potential. Their lack of pretense is refreshing, and their propensity to demonstrate their faith without reserve makes me love them all the more.

But that's not why I applied to be a youth intern at Fairfield Baptist Church in Cypress, Texas. In between my freshman and sophomore years in college, I wanted to see where I could fit on a church staff and if vocational ministry might be in my future. Thank goodness Joey Dodson was the youth pastor who hired me as one of his interns; anyone else, and I might not still be serving Christ today.

Joey was the first Christian male leader to give me a chance, and unexpectedly, he treated me like an equal. He gave me a seat at his ministry table, and I started to believe Jesus' mission included me, even though I was "just" a woman. Joey hired me to be the girls' youth intern, but a few weeks after my start date, he moved to Arkansas, where he would pastor and become a seminary professor. You'd think a few weeks with him as my boss wouldn't leave such an impression on me, but it did. Just last week a new church member and I connected via social media because we both learned about Jesus through Joey's teaching. It's two decades later, and still I'm meeting women in ministry who can link their current position of service to his admonition to pursue Jesus with their all. Many of us share similar sentiments. Had it not been for Dr. Dodson, we might not still be in the faith, let alone in leadership roles.

Joey's intentionality to include me in every meeting concerning the youth ministry changed me. I sat next to Ryan, the boys' youth intern, while Joey led us through Scripture readings, strategy planning, and prayer. It seemed as though Ryan and I would have parallel positions, something I didn't expect. As I dreamed about how to invest in the lives of the girls at our church, I never anticipated that ministry to the girls would get equal consideration as the ministry to the boys. Long before "shared leadership" would be a thing, Joey passed his position as youth pastor on to Ryan and me to colead the youth group. There was no fuss about it; that's just the way it was.

If I were to trace the undoing of my incorrect limitations of the role of women, I'd see the thread came loose when Joey invited me to be a leader. Like the unraveling of a knit scarf, his radical inclusion untangled some of my constricted views about how women fit into God's ministry plans.

The thing is, Joey was just emulating Jesus' example in the Bible of how to treat women. From the beginning of time, God has relentlessly included women in the story of redemption and elevated women's voices in countercultural ways. While Moses struggled with confidence, Miriam boldly led the nation of Israel in worship after their deliverance from the Red Sea. Although not one good male judge can be found ruling over God's people in the book of Judges, Deborah is presented in the narrative as the wise prophetess, speaking on behalf of God; a successful warrior in battle, securing wins against Israel's enemies; and a wise judge, ruling fairly in the government's highest office. A woman in the Bible was the first to be Christ's disciple (Mary of Nazareth), missionary (woman at the well), evangelist (woman at the well), and gospel preacher (Mary Magdalene). Our faith history is rich with radical female figures living faith-filled lives of courage and devotion. All of this in spite of the patriarchy that defined their reality.

God works overtime in the Scriptures to confirm what he has said since our genesis in Genesis: women matter to God. This is not to say women are better than men—not even close. It seems my attempts to value women in the same way God does in the Bible are often interpreted as a knock against men or having a bone to pick. The opposite is true. I don't believe "the future is female," as some do, with an agenda to slight our brothers in Christ. Instead, I want the Scriptures to inform how we see women, encourage women, value women, celebrate and include women, all with the assumption that doing so will enable Christians, men and women, to fulfill the great command to love God with our everything. The future is male *and* female, as God designed. Much like how God reverses the cultural norms for women in the Bible, the Christian men I know who are supporting their sisters in Christ are also fighting against the world's view of women. I, for one, want to be known as the Bible teacher who is constantly reminding you that most of our brothers in Jesus are standing firm in their convictions that we belong in God's work as their partners in advancing the gospel. That's why I want to celebrate the Joey Dodsons—and why I can't get over the way Jesus treated the woman at the well in John 4.

We've established that Jesus' must-have conversation with the woman at the well was the purpose of his stop in Samaria, and his stop changed the narrative about women at wells. We saw Jesus on mission, coming near to the Samaritan woman in her mess, delighting in making her broken place a sacred space.

Now let's take a closer look at the scandalous ways Jesus

includes women in his story of redemption. Jesus crossed gender lines, broke social norms, and defied ethnic boundaries, and so should we.

Countless conversations with women lead me to believe that a lot of us feel like outsiders. Sometimes it's a single comment from a parent that cuts us to the quick, leaving a scar we bear daily. Sometimes it's being let go from a job, enduring a miscarriage, or experiencing an empty nest that makes us feel as if we are no longer in the majority, part of the club, or enjoying the inside. Feelings of exclusion have devastating effects on our lives.

From your viewpoint, you might be on the outside looking in. But you're not alone. The woman at the well knew a thing or two about exclusion and isolation because of her gender, social class, and ethnicity.

Belonging is God's work. Contrary to what our circumstances might be communicating to us, no one and nothing can keep us away from God's love. You, my friend, belong—even when you feel like an outsider or experience exclusion.

I'm convinced that some of our in-between places in life can be so isolating that they leave us wondering if we are any good to anybody. I'm here to remind you, and myself, that Jesus' countercultural methods mean that no one gets left out of his mission. You are not disqualified from participating in building the kingdom with your gifts, talents, and treasures because of your age, stage, title, relationship status, race, gender, or class. Anywhere God is at work, men and women belong. And the beautiful thing is, he is *everywhere*.

As we review the Samaritan woman's position in her

world—a low-class citizen, the wrong gender, a despised ethnicity—we will see that in Jesus everyone belongs, and our job is to extend that belonging to everyone.

CREATING SPACES WHERE EVERYONE BELONGS

"Would you like some champagne?"

Dr. Sandra Glahn, seminary professor at Dallas Theological Seminary, wanted to toast my book deal while she treated me to lunch. She's one of those door-opening leaders who wave women into their callings. She wanted to hear my publishing story, and I couldn't wait to tell her. As usual, Aaron was the one who first encouraged me to write, and so Sandi and I clinked our bubbly in honor of Aaron Armstrong's advocacy for women. That prompted Sandi to tell me a story about Aaron—one I'd never heard.

Apparently, Aaron found refuge in Sandi's office at the seminary one day after a demoralizing class with a different professor. Aaron recounted the topic of the day: Should women be allowed to vote? Aaron laughed out loud, thinking the prompt was a joke. But to his horror, many folks in his class argued against women being able to vote. Yes, this was in this century. And yes, this was a conversation among Christians. Let that sink in. Aaron found himself debating folks contending that women were better off *without* so much liberty. Next thing he knew, he was in Sandi's office wiping tears away as he grieved over the misogyny that has such a foothold among future Christian leaders.

Sandi and I were at lunch celebrating new doors being opened to women in the publishing world, and yet we spent a lot of our time together swapping stories about how hard-fought progress had come. What Aaron thought was ancient history was, sadly, still present.

Jesus' conversation with someone of the "wrong" gender proves that women matter to God as much as our brothers in Christ do. And not only was he talking to a woman; he was about to teach her theology—which was in some circles a big no-no.

My friend Nika Spaulding, the resident theologian of the St. Jude Oak Cliff church in Oak Cliff, Texas, summarized in a paper some important aspects of Jesus' conversation with the nameless Samaritan woman: "Pious Jews lived in fear of inter-acting with women" because women were viewed as threats to one's purity. As a result, devout Jewish men avoided encoun-ters with women. So when "Jesus chose to engage this woman in public at a well, he established a different norm. Rather than viewing the woman as a potential threat to his sexual purity, Jesus enters into a platonic conversation regarding spiritual matters."[1]

Jesus' example overturned centuries of misogynistic avoidance of women. Instead of ignoring her out of fear of his ritual purity or what other people would think, Jesus' actions confirm that women are worthy of our attention and investment.

The fear that began with Jewish religious leaders trans-ferred into centuries of continued misogynistic teachings, as evidenced by the following summary of some of Christianity's greatest leaders and their demeaning views of women. I'm indebted to theologian Marg Mowczko for compiling most of this list.[2] First on her list, the renowned "Father of Latin Christianity," Tertullian, taught that women were the "devil's gateway."[3] Thomas Aquinas, priest and philosopher in the thirteenth century, taught that women were inherently defective.[4] Martin Luther, a German priest, theologian, and Protestant reformer, taught that women did not equal the glory God gave to men.[5] Augustine taught that women's only purpose was to help men in procreation and to bear children.[6]

I'd like to add to this blooper reel what pastor and bestselling author John Piper has said. He believes women are "more gullible or deceivable than men and therefore less fit for the doctrinal oversight of the church."[7] Before his fall from grace, famous megachurch pastor Mark Driscoll was instrumental in cofounding several influential evangelical organizations, including the Resurgence, Acts 29 network, and the Gospel Coalition. He also taught that women are unfit to lead in church "because they are more gullible and easier to deceive than men."[8] Most recently, famed John MacArthur made Beth Moore the butt of his jokes during a seminary chapel service, suggesting that she should "go home" and that representation of diversity in Bible translation is ridiculous.[9]

As troubling as it may be to review, generations of respected church leaders and theologians with misogynistic views have influenced the way we read Scripture and internalize truth. They got a lot right; they just got a lot wrong too. No wonder women struggle to find where we fit in service to God and as a help to others. No wonder our hearts ache for assurance that we will find our way to bring God glory and to work toward the common good of all people. How can we find our place if we are spending all our energy trying to stay inside the imaginary lines that have been drawn to limit the use of our spiritual gifts?

A lot of us feel left out because we are. We've been excluded on purpose. Yes, one could have biblical convictions on limiting women's roles at home, the workplace, or ministry. But as we can see so clearly from our early and current church fathers—the ones who have had the most influence over Bible interpretation and praxis—they were not only constrained by a limitation on a woman's role in ministry; unfortunately, some of their misapplications have been willful misogyny. The irony is that believing women are a threat to the world is the real threat to God's intention for all his image bearers, men and women, to be all in for Jesus. God has a plan for all of us. Everyone counts. Everyone matters.

Nika perfectly summarized the way Jesus upset the social-norm system. She said, "Jews during [the time of Christ's conversation with the woman at the well] refused to share utensils with Samaritans due to the enmity between them."[10] The Mishnah, a book of the oral traditions of Jewish law, states, "The daughters of Samaritans are menstruants from their cradles."[11] Nika's scholarship on the story of the woman at the well reminds me that according to Leviticus 15:19, all menstruating women were considered unclean, and whoever touched those women also became unclean. Being "unclean" was not just a matter of washing one's hands before a meal, as we are used to doing. No, being "unclean" in this woman's era meant being unable to participate in spiritual activities and religious rituals. And the unclean were to be shunned. To talk with a Samaritan, let alone ask to share a water jug, paints a picture of guilt by association.

Not only did Jesus ignore the clear teachings of the day; he took it one step further with his willingness to share a water jug with the woman at the well. The religious leaders of the Samaritan woman's day believed that "uncleanliness spread through touching a vessel from which a woman drank."[12] Clearly put, Jesus' request for a drink from the woman at the well "defied several societal norms."[13]

Ben Witherington, my favorite American New Testament scholar, says, "Jesus not only speaks to the woman, but carries on a lengthy and theologically profound discussion with her, violating Jewish custom."[14] Witherington writes, "If one is going to preach or teach this text [John 4] adequately, it will be necessary to stress the intentionality of Jesus and of God in reaching across lines, and to stress the way Jesus enables even despised and disfranchised people like Samaritans *and* women to become disciples and *able* witnesses for the Savior in the world" (emphasis added).[15]

Jesus' radical move across gender and social boundaries signaled that his mission welcomed everyone—even a woman living in the scorned Samaria—into his kingdom. In fact, she would become the first to testify about Jesus. She meant something to Jesus. And so do we. Enough to risk his reputation and, eventually, to offer up his life to save ours.

Before Gail R. O'Day passed in 2018, her scholarly research focused on the gospel of John, preaching, and the history of biblical interpretation. She wrote a number of books and articles, including the commentary on the gospel of John in *The New Interpreter's Bible*, and one of the most succinct and powerful summaries of John 4 in the *Women's Bible Commentary*. O'Day was quick to point out the contrast we've already made note of, that right before Jesus talked with the Samaritan woman, he talked with a "male member of the Jewish religious establishment."[16] But in John 4, Jesus spoke with a female member of "an enemy people." In the next chapter we will explore why Jews and Samaritans hated each other. For now, I want you to see that the woman at the well herself noted the scandal of her conversation with Jesus when she said, "How is it that you, a Jew, ask a drink of me, a Samaritan woman?" (v. 9 NRSV). When Jesus' disciples returned from their food run to find Jesus midconversation with a Samaritan woman, they were "astonished" (v. 27 NRSV). O'Day pointed out, "Their protests reflect traditional cultural and social conventions and expectations, and their protests show their distance from Jesus and his work in the world."[17] God's "chosen" people shouldn't and wouldn't associate with God's "rejected" people, but Jesus' demonstration is that the grace of God is for all. So long, status quo. Bye-bye, wall of hostility. Hello, oneness.

The apostle Paul spent a lot of space in his letter to the Christians living in Ephesus talking about the way Jesus could unify two groups of people, the Jews and Gentiles (Eph. 2:11–22). Paul explained that exclusion meant being an outsider in terms of citizenship in Israel and the promises of God made to Israel. Exclusion meant living without hope. The solution to close the distance was Jesus, who has the power to bring those who are far away near to his presence, promises, and hope. Jesus fused the two groups together by tearing down the hostile divisions.

The cost of reconciliation? Jesus' death. Now those who follow Christ all have equal access to God. No one, the Bible says, can be a Christian and be shut out. This one new group, made from two, was suddenly being built together for God's purpose.

This is not the only place the apostle Paul used his New Testament letters to emphasize the transformative unity Christ brings in spite of our differences with one another. In his letter to the Christians in Galatia he wrote, "There is no Jew or Greek, slave or free, male and female; since you are all one in Christ Jesus" (Gal. 3:28). His hyperbole was not to say that our ethnic, social, or gender differences are not important or interchangeable, but rather, in Christ, we can all be one.

Dr. Brené Brown makes the point in her book *The Gifts of Imperfection* that fitting in and belonging are two very different things. Whereas fitting in is about assimilating to our surroundings, belonging "doesn't require us to change who we are; it requires us to be who we are."[18] She argues that belonging is as essential to the human experience as love. She defines belonging as "the innate human desire to be a part of something larger than us. Because this yearning is so primal, we often try to acquire it by fitting in and by seeking approval, which are not only hollow substitutes for belonging, but often barriers to it."[19]

In Jesus, the work of belonging has been accomplished for us through his life, death, and resurrection. But I wonder if we resist opting into something God is clearly directing us to because we've been left out too many times. Whether it's being erased, silenced, cautioned, or looked over, I know those wounds are all too real. Let's welcome Jesus' healing in those areas of our lives so we can be released from approval seeking and be commissioned into gospel sharing.

GRACE GUIDES BELONGING

In between my start and finish at Dallas Seminary, smack-dab in the middle of what turned out to be eight years into a two-year degree program, I registered for one of Dr. Glenn Kreider's theology courses. I would have to ask the school to pull my transcript to help me remember just how many courses I took with Dr. Kreider and which credit hours were fulfilled under his teaching. But for now, what I can remember is that after that first class, I reworked my schedule as best as possible, even with full-time work hours, to get into his classes when they were offered. If he was teaching a class, I wanted to be in it. His sarcasm is razor sharp and keeps his classes' attention, and I'm partial to his musical choices when pairing a music lyric or video to a biblical teaching. This is code for "he can be trusted because he loves U2 more than I do."

In Dr. Kreider's ecclesiology class, a class about the study of the church, I found myself in the midst of a heated class conversation about the role of women in the church. One of the students commented that he didn't understand why so much hot air was wasted on the topic. "Let's get on with it already," the student mused. I suggested that if he had been born a woman, he would care more about the nuances. If part of his understanding of self and his place within a local church body depended upon the Scriptures' teaching on women's participation, he would care deeply.

After class I emailed Dr. Kreider to share that I felt diminished by the interaction. I'm not sure if I was motivated to write him because I was looking for compassion or correction or absolution, but his response forever changed me. He apologized. He asked for my forgiveness for not creating a more inclusive atmosphere for everyone in the room.

In the same way I hadn't expected Dr. Joey Dodson to treat me like an equal as a youth intern, I didn't expect Dr. Glenn Kreider to apologize or become my spiritual father as the years went on. Maybe, had I been a better student of the Scriptures or more willing to belong where I'd been called, I would have seen their acts of grace toward me as the normal way we should all treat one another. Maybe I would have connected their partnership in gospel work as God's design and the way of Jesus.

As I struggled to figure out which degree program fit my needs, which direction I would go after graduation, and if I was even cut out for ministry, God used Dr. Kreider's voice in my life time and time again to keep me moving forward with confidence. When I moved out of my in-between season of learning about my faith into an extended season of practicing my faith, I started to see a pattern. The men most closely aligned to the Word of God were some of the fiercest advocates for including women in all the rooms where decisions are made. Like Jesus, men who invite women to pull up a chair in the home, neighborhood, marketplace, academy, and church are simply living up to God's radical belonging-ness.

We see interdependence modeled in the New Testament church through the apostle Paul's partnership with women to build the church; this should be our standard while navigating our in-between places. This is why we shouldn't "show up for ourselves" but rather give in to Jesus and co-labor alongside our brothers and sisters in Jesus.

Discussion Questions

1. Describe a time when you felt you belonged.
2. When do you feel most excluded?
3. What gender roles do you need to cross to help more people embrace belonging?
4. What social class norms do you need to break to help more people embrace belonging?
5. What ethnic divides do you need to bridge to help more people embrace belonging?
6. How significant do you think it is that the woman at the well was the first to testify about Jesus?

Study Guide

Visit www.katarmstrong.com/theinbetweenplace to download the free study guide. Materials for chapter 5 include

- quotes from Nika Spaulding's paper
- Marg Mowczko's list of church father quotes
- my graduation picture with Dr. Kreider

SIX

STOP SHOWING UP
FOR YOURSELF

Our failures or successes in the Christian life
are not what define us or determine our worth
before God or God's people. Instead, we are
defined by Christ's life and work on our behalf.

—TISH HARRISON WARREN

This is not like other Sundays.

With Aaron on his annual July sabbatical, Caleb and I
decided to attend our home church like normal. But everything about this Sunday turned out to be unusual.

There is an unavoidable element of feeling on call when
serving in the ministry. Aaron practices healthy boundaries,

manages his time carefully, and doesn't sacrifice the well-being of our family. But his role as pastor is consuming, and it's rare that someone calls him after hours to encourage him with happy news. When he gets multiple texts all at one time, we know there's an emergency with a church member.

To offset the demands of his job, Aaron takes a monthlong vacation every July. Resting looks different for everybody. For me, resting is reading a good book. For Caleb, it's LEGOs; for Aaron, it's visiting other churches. Yes, you read that right. Aaron is passionate not just about his own congregation; he loves the universal church. On a sabbatical Sunday he might visit as many as three different churches in our city. So on this particular Sunday, when Caleb and I went to our home church by ourselves, Aaron took communion with the Anglicans at 8:00 a.m., sang hymns at a traditional Baptist church at 9:30 a.m., and then danced with a black church at 11:00 a.m. He always comes home on top of the world after seeing the way our sisters and brothers are worshiping and serving our city. Little did he know he'd come home that day to celebrate a new member of the body of Christ—his very own son.

I'm sure our church had sent out several notifications, but vacationing with Aaron for a few weeks had left us disoriented. We were unknowingly walking into a family Sunday, a time when Dallas Bible Church suspends weekly kids' ministry to include children and youth in "big church." Everything is geared to make the tiny humans feel included and connected to the broader life of the church; it's beautiful. I was trying to punch into the check-in system in the kids' area but kept getting an error message. It took me a minute to realize that no one was in the children's hallway. Then the thought occurred to me: *This is not like other Sundays.*

Four weeks earlier Caleb's reading skills had throttled into lightning speed after months of puttering through sight-reading. A gear must have shifted because he went from struggling to get through a book without frustration to gleefully asking if he could read to me aloud. Caleb was partially motivated toward a reading breakthrough because he wanted to know the artists singing the songs in the car. He could see the car dashboard populate the song title and artist name, but it would change so quickly that he wouldn't have time to figure out what it said. Music is important to me. And it's becoming important to Caleb, too, because this is the Lord's will for his life. *Wink.*

When Caleb was just one month old, I created a music calendar to make sure we helped his brain form a refined musical palette. We spent a whole month working through the U2 catalog. I am not joking. When we are not listening to U2, the greatest rock band of all time, the car station is tuned to Christian music.

That unusual Sunday morning, when Caleb and I sat down in the sanctuary, he quickly leaned over and whispered in my ear, "Mommy, I can read all the slides!" Together we glanced up at the screens near the front of the auditorium to read the words of the worship song being sung and then quickly gave each other a smileful eye lock. Caleb was giddy. His ability to sing along was a significant moment in his little life. He looked so proud mouthing the words to the songs and following the cues of our worship minister. To top it all off, Caleb's elementary minister, Mr. Zane, was preaching in Aaron's absence. As soon as Mr. Zane walked up to the microphone, Caleb gasped, "Mr. Zane!" *This is not like other Sundays.*

For the last few months, Caleb and I had been having deep theological conversations. His interest in the gospel, that Jesus loves us and wants to be in a relationship with us through his life, death, and resurrection, had been piqued. It seemed as though every day he had new and hard-to-answer questions for me about the Christian faith. I could tell that, like the gears on some of his building sets, his mind was turning over big concepts like forgiveness, salvation, and repentance. Most of the questions were prompted after listening to a song in the car. While he was trying to process popular song lyrics like "I raise a hallelujah" or "the darkness can't hide," I was trying to teach him the difference between literal meaning and metaphorical meaning.

Metaphors serve to help us understand really big concepts. When our words are deficient, we paint a picture with our words. Leland Ryken, in his book *How to Read the Bible as Literature*, notes that "metaphor and simile place immense demands on a reader. They require far more activity than a direct propositional statement. Metaphor and simile first demand that we take the time to let the literal situation sink in. Then we must make a transfer of meaning to the topic or experience.... They are one way of overcoming the limitations of abstraction."[1] As holy moments presented themselves, I'd take every opportunity to ask Caleb if he was ready to become a Christian. Until this Sunday, he'd answered matter-of-factly no. I appreciated his self-awareness and resolved each time to ask again when the moment seemed right.

As we sang the final song in the service, Caleb started inching toward me, almost snuggling with me. This was unusual too. As the pastor's kid, he's usually raring to run around the sanctuary as soon as the worship concludes. In Caleb's world, church dismissal is like waving the checkered flag. He's typically bounding up the steps of the stage to sneak into the drummer's cage or give his daddy a big hug. But not this Sunday. Instead, he was nestled next to me, totally tuned in to the moment. The words *ask again* kept coming to my mind, so I leaned over and whispered in Caleb's ear, "Are you ready to become a Christian today?" He bit his lip with a weepy smile and nodded yes. But he was quick to say he didn't want to do it at church; he wanted to talk at home.

Although we only live a mile away from church, I floored it through our neighborhood. I couldn't get home soon enough.

The dilemma then became, should I have this life-changing conversation with Caleb before Aaron got home or wait? Aaron had texted he was going in to worship with his black brothers and sisters and not to wait on him for lunch. Ultimately I decided to lean into this sacred opportunity and talk to Caleb about following Jesus. Just the two of us, we sat on our couch and talked about why he wanted to make a profession of faith.

The conversation I had with Caleb that day on the couch had a lot to do with Jesus' ongoing presence in our lives. Although the phrase "Jesus coming into your heart" is woefully deficient to describe how God is a part of our lives and bodies, to a first grader it's accessible enough to conceive of God becoming a part of us forever.

Jesus' conversation with the woman at the well centers on a metaphor about God's sustaining presence in our lives: living water. Thankfully, we have Christ's teaching to help us understand his metaphor when he said he could offer her living water to drink. I think Christ's point to the Samaritan woman in John 4 is that we need living water to make up for all the cracks in our character and gaps in our in-between places. Implied in the living water lesson is that we need a constant source of renewable water because we are broken cisterns. The good news is that when we can't show up for ourselves and it feels like no one is able to get into the crevasses of our in-between places, Jesus will always show up for us. We can count on his presence, always.

WE ARE BROKEN CISTERNS

Living water was not a new concept for God's people; although, up until Jesus' conversation with the woman at the well, they might have been more acquainted with the broken cistern part of the metaphor. Jeremiah used related imagery all throughout his prophetic book, which happens to be the longest book in the whole Bible. More words are used in that book than any other,[2] which triggers a reminder that Jesus' conversation with the Samaritan woman is the longest recorded in the New Testament. There is space in God's Word to discuss how messed up we are and the solutions he's provided for our rescue, and that seems to indicate just how serious God is about our well-being.

In chapter 1 of his book, Jeremiah was called by God to speak on God's behalf as a prophet. Understandably, Jeremiah was scared. Maybe it was his young age, or that God was talking to him, or that his primary function in his generation would be to "uproot and tear down, to destroy and demolish, to build and plant" (Jer. 1:10). Jeremiah's pronouncements to the people of God were all judgment and impending doom. He was consistently exhorting God's people to repent, knowing that God, in his omnipotence, allows us to experience the consequences of our sin. Many scholars refer to Jeremiah as the "weeping prophet," and I think his mournful wrestling with God as well as his troubling occupation to announce terrible punishment led to his reputation as the prophet who wept. But in light of our journey to follow Jesus to Shechem, I am reminded that Jeremiah's tears are connected on a deeper level to our observations about living water.

Disregarding all God's laws, his people had rebelled and brought upon themselves God's rebuke. Although God graciously warned and instructed the Israelites regarding how to live, they chose not to follow his ways. Instead, they unrepentantly defied God. Keep in mind, God's judgments against them were just, because he had been über-clear about the difference between right and wrong. Start in Genesis, read all the way through to Jeremiah, and tally up how many times God did everything *but* punish his people in the midst of their sin. Just as a loving parent cautions his children to stop their behavior before they have to experience consequences, God sent another prophet, Jeremiah, to get people's attention—if they would just listen.

According to Jeremiah 2:13, God's accusations against the Israelites were twofold. One, they had "abandoned" God, "the fountain of living water." And second, they had "dug cisterns for themselves—cracked cisterns that cannot hold water." God is the only being able to replenish our needs. He's the only one who can stabilize us from our dysfunction. He's the only one powerful enough to sustain our every breath.

Like the Israelites, we, too, abandon God for self-help propaganda. It seems like everyone on earth has something to say, or should I say *sell*, that promises a better life, when the Author of life himself has already made it clear that living in good standing with him is all we need for life and godliness. We have everything we need in Jesus. When our attempts to solve our own problems or go our own way don't pan out, it's only natural to try to fix our mistakes ourselves. That's why the Israelites had dug their own cisterns.

When we reject God's provision as the fountain of living water, we have to make our own water supply, and it's always a pitiful failure. Why? Cracked cisterns can't hold water.

You and I are like cracked cisterns, and so are the systems of the world. Our relationships, body image, and goals are all fractured by sin. We can't escape our humanity. But the water we need to keep us alive and hydrated will escape through our in-betweens if we are not supplied by a renewable water source.

It's hard to get from one chapter to the next in Jeremiah's book without noticing the recurring theme of broken cisterns. In chapter 18, God asked Jeremiah to go to a potter's house and watch him work at the wheel while God revealed new words to Jeremiah. Watching the potter shape a lump of clay into a jar kept Jeremiah's attention even when the jar became flawed in the potter's hands. The potter took the defective clay jar and changed its shape altogether. This object lesson was followed by God's statement that he would treat the Israelites like a clay vessel he was fashioning into something that could hold water, but their flaws caused him to reshape their future.

The symbolism of the potter's work in chapter 18 is followed by a project God gives to Jeremiah in chapter 19 to buy a clay jar, gather up the leaders of the city, and prophesy their coming judgment. Just another day at the office for Jeremiah. At the end of his prophetic word to the people, he was instructed to shatter the jar of clay in their presence and then teach everyone that God had the power to shatter the people and the city in such a way that the broken vessel couldn't be repaired. The imagery would have been very uncomfortable for them. It certainly is for me. I don't like experiencing the consequences of my sin.

Coming full circle, the story of the woman at the well in John 4 connected to not only Dinah's rape in Genesis 34 but also a story the prophet Jeremiah relates later in Jeremiah 41. This section of Jeremiah's book follows what happened to God's people after they were overtaken by the Babylonians, captured, and exiled.

In a matter of a few paragraphs, Jeremiah summarized how their greatest fear had come true: Jerusalem fell. I have to intentionally pause when I read the tragedy. A whole people group was overpowered by evil rulers. It feels all too close to home when I consider that their captivity was a result of their own mistakes, mistakes they had been warned about over and over. Their lives had been ruined. God's people would suffer under tyrants and be displaced from their homes for many years to come. Destined to return to the promised land, the Israelites often found themselves in the liminal, or in-between, space of *not there yet*. Exile is one of the hardest in-between places in the story of God's people.

Near the end of the book, the prophet Jeremiah told the story of a wicked Babylonian ruler named Ishmael who was hunting a man named Gedaliah, who had been charged with overseeing the remnant of Israelites allowed to stay in Judah. Ishmael sounds a lot like the other evil rulers we've read about so far. He was ruthless, power hungry, and deceptive. Ishmael successfully killed Gedaliah, and then the day after Gedaliah's murder, eighty men from Samaria—more specifically, Shechem—came to the temple with their offerings. Yup, they were from the same place Dinah was raped, the same place of Jesus' future encounter with the woman at the well. *Shechem*. The eighty men from Samaria had no idea Gedaliah was dead or that Ishmael would cause their demise. According to Jeremiah 41:7, Ishmael slaughtered most of the group and then threw the bodies into a cistern. Not only did evil happen *in* Shechem; it followed those *from* Shechem.

When I retold this part of the Israelite story to a Sunday school class at Dallas Bible Church, many wanted to contribute to our conversation by offering their life stories to the group. We talked about life after divorce, life after loss, and living through constant loneliness. It was as if the whole room collectively groaned as each classmate described different ways lives had been shattered. All our stories were unique, but the shared experiences of grieving our in-between places superseded the differences.

Our conclusion? Life is fragile. The breaking of our hopes and dreams can be so painful, especially when we feel as if we are left with the task of picking up the pieces ourselves. At the end of class, one person bravely expressed how comforting it felt to be in a room full of people willing to admit they had experienced some hard knocks. The break in her voice came as she stated that our hope in Jesus is tangible when we are gathered together sharing stories with each other. She was describing the gift of presence.

JESUS IS LIVING WATER

Let's go back to the well for a moment, in John 4:10–14. The first thing Jesus said to the woman at the well was "Give me a drink" (v. 7). Shocked by the scandal of the request, she tried to figure out Jesus' motivation for it. Jesus fired right back by telling her that if she knew who he was, she wouldn't have questions; she would be asking for living water.

We're not sure whether she was incredulous or feisty, but we do know she pointed out that what Jesus was asking of her was not possible. He didn't have a bucket, number one, and number two, the well was deep. But beyond that, what was this living water he was talking about? She clearly didn't understand. Still stuck on the physical well in front of them, she brought up Jacob's name. He was the well's original owner, so she was wondering if Jesus was trying to tell her that he was superior to Jacob because of what he could offer her.

Though you and I might understand what Jesus was talking about, put yourself in her shoes. She was confused. She knew he was referring to something else beyond literal water, but she couldn't quite figure it out. What was this different kind of water that could satisfy your thirst for now but also quench your thirst forever?

Jesus was of course talking about a spiritual thirst. And yes, not only is he better than the original well owner, but he has the power to create wells in our souls that are perpetually full of this living water.

So important is the message, Jesus taught on it further a few chapters later in John 7, when he was talking to some Jews living in Jerusalem. In John 7:37–39, he cried out to the people listening to his teaching and said that anyone who was thirsty should come to him for a drink. How does someone get the living water? By believing in Jesus as Messiah. The result? They will have "streams of living water flow from deep within" them (v. 38).

Not only are streams of living water available to us, no matter how broken a cistern we are, but we can also hold and dispense water because a relationship with Christ means our broken vessels become wells.

Sometimes we must let go of something to make our transition from a broken cistern to a living well. When I asked our class what they needed to exchange for Jesus' living water, several said they needed to let go of the thirst they had to grow their CV for their career in academics. Others needed to trade the praise of their colleagues for Jesus' ongoing presence. One person said she was thirsting for security. Every day was another opportunity to worry wildly about her children, and she desperately wanted to know they were safe from all harm. She wanted to exchange her desire to control circumstances for the living water, Jesus' protection. The person who admitted to being lonely said she felt so alone in her circumstances, like no one could really understand, but she was done with trying to fill that need in her life just with compassionate people; she wanted more of Jesus.

Before we closed class, we turned to Revelation 7, another place where John wrote about Jesus as the living water. The tender moment lent itself to these words: "The Lamb who is at the center of the throne will shepherd them; he will guide them to springs of the waters of life, and God will wipe away every tear from their eyes" (v. 17). I wonder if God is wiping happy or sad tears away in Revelation 7. I imagine for the Samaritan woman it was both. Tears of lament over the way God's image bearers, herself included, had been treated in Samaria, and tears of unspeakable joy because her soul would never thirst again.

It's important to recognize that God wipes our tears away. It's not "Stop crying and wipe *your* tears away." We can trust God to help us, even when others might be telling us to figure it out on our own and fix our own problems.

This "show up for yourself" trend fills memes galore, and the people digesting this alluring form of self-help chug it as if it's the last drink they'll ever have. Just be more attuned to your own needs, they say. Just put yourself first more often, they say. Our problem, they think, is that when it comes to our own lives, we're not committed to our own success. Hear me: I get the need to balance the martyr syndrome so many suffer under with a healthy dose of self-care. I do. But what makes me super uncomfortable is knowing that most will read suggestions to "show up for yourself" and then try to dig a well for themselves, like the people Jeremiah chastised.

I think a generation of women are sick and tired, literally, of doing more, trying harder, and making self-help an idol. Jesus offers us just the help we need.

One of the ways Jesus changes our stories in our in-between places is *not* by handing us a shovel and pointing to a place to dig a cistern in the ground. Jesus shows up for us and dares us to ask him for a drink, to let him be our well. If your broken self has trouble supplying your every need, it's because you're on a fool's errand. Stop trying to show up for yourself; Jesus does that best.

How do we stop trying to show up for ourselves? One way is by admitting our weakness to trusted friends, or asking our spiritual mentors for guidance and prayer. We could schedule time with a spiritual director or book an appointment with a licensed professional counselor. We could email our small group and list a few things we could use some help with. We could finally cave and hire a housekeeper to come and help when we need it most. We could tell someone who asks how we are doing the nuanced, complicated truth. Probably one of the most powerful ways we could let God be our living water is to ask him to be our main source of encouragement and strength.

RECKLESS LOVE

Caleb and I plopped onto our tufted leather couch in the living room to talk about the unique Sunday we'd had together while I racked my brain over how to boil down the basics of the Christian faith for my six-year-old son. He'd known all the right answers for months, but this conversation wasn't so much about the answers as it was about his faith. I wanted to convey four core truths:

1. God launched the human project to see us flourish as God's vice-regents here on earth.
2. But all of us suffer under broken systems and relationships because of sin.
3. Through a relationship with Jesus we can confess our sins to God, repent of our ways, and receive forgiveness for messing up God's project.
4. Someday God is going to come back and make all things new and right all wrongs.

So I synthesized the same truths by sharing the "big story" of the Bible.

1. God made something good.
2. We messed it up.
3. Jesus makes it right.
4. One day God will make all things new.

Familiar with these phrases, Caleb kept nodding his head and saying these truths with me. I spent most of our time talking about the time between Jesus making things right and God making all things new. That's where we live our lives, in between the resurrection of Christ and the complete redemption of the whole world. I tried my best to instill in my son that life with Jesus does not keep us from feeling like broken water jars or from the pieces falling apart. Instead, life with Jesus means he's always with us, even in the in-betweens of life.

Caleb got it. Not only did he internalize these truths; they became his own. When I asked why he wanted to become a Christian, he said, "I want Jesus to be mine." Tear my heart out, why don't you? The moment felt holy, totally set apart. Caleb prayed to receive Christ, and right after he opened his eyes he said, "Mommy, my happy feelings are too big for my heart; they're coming out of my eyes!"

No sooner had I wiped my own tears away than he asked if I could play "Reckless Love" on my phone. He said, "Can we just sit here and listen together?" By some miracle I was able to hold back tears of joy and, with blurred eyes, scroll through my phone to find one of Caleb's favorite summer songs. The lyrics paint a picture of a God who won't let anything come between his beloved children and his presence: "No shadow he won't light up, no mountain he won't climb up coming after me."[3]

Why does God go through these extreme lengths to be near to us? Because of his overwhelming, never-ending love. As Cory Asbury's words washed over us, we held hands and took a video for Daddy. When Aaron got home from his Dallas church tour, he burst through the door to scoop up Caleb with a super-tight squeeze. He needed all the details.

"We have videos for you, Daddy," Caleb reported.

Team Armstrong huddled around the phone screen to replay the living water filling up Caleb's life.

Discussion Questions

1. If your life is represented by a broken cistern, what created the cracks?
2. Describe a time when you felt as if your life dreams were shattered.
3. How did you pick up the pieces?
4. What about Jesus' ongoing presence in your life brings you comfort when life is broken?
5. What do you thirst for most in life?
6. How is Jesus a better thirst quencher than your normal go-to fixes?

Study Guide

Visit www.katarmstrong.com/theinbetweenplace to download the free study guide. Materials for chapter 6 include

- a book recommendation about God's presence with us
- pictures of Caleb's conversion moment
- the big story of the Bible

PART 2 SUMMARY

Together we've looked at John 4:6–18, taking with us three crucial truths about finding hope in our present.

1. We need to share our story with safe people. Our companions during our journey are important for any in-between place. Although Jesus already knew the woman at the well's story, he asked to hear it, and in sharing her life with Jesus, she was truly seen and loved. We can emulate God's example by entrusting our journeys to trustworthy people along the way, especially Jesus.

2. Embracing belonging will clear our heads and hearts of any negative or distracting feelings of being left out of God's work. Jesus went to great lengths to show us how we should treat one another, even going so far as

to overturn widely held beliefs about who is in and who is out of God's kingdom. We need to not only be a part of God's family but also share that radical and inclusive love with everyone we meet—because everyone belongs.

3. Showing up for ourselves is helpful only as long as we recognize Jesus as the sustaining power in our lives. Finding hope in our present is deeply connected to our resilience and fortitude, both of which only God can provide with his presence in our lives through the Holy Spirit.

PART THREE

STEP CONFIDENTLY INTO YOUR FUTURE

Jesus said to her, "Go, call your husband, and come back." The woman answered him, "I have no husband." Jesus said to her, "You are right in saying, 'I have no husband'; for you have had five husbands, and the one you have now is not your husband. What you have said is true!" The woman said to him, "Sir, I see that you are a prophet. Our ancestors worshiped on this mountain, but you say that the place where people must worship is in Jerusalem." Jesus said to her, "Woman, believe me, the hour is coming when you will worship the Father neither on this mountain nor in Jerusalem. You worship what you do not know;

we worship what we know, for salvation is from the Jews. But the hour is coming, and is now here, when the true worshipers will worship the Father in spirit and truth, for the Father seeks such as these to worship him. God is spirit, and those who worship him must worship in spirit and truth." The woman said to him, "I know that Messiah is coming" (who is called Christ). "When he comes, he will proclaim all things to us." Jesus said to her, "I am he, the one who is speaking to you."

Just then his disciples came. They were astonished that he was speaking with a woman, but no one said, "What do you want?" or, "Why are you speaking with her?" Then the woman left her water jar and went back to the city. She said to the people, "Come and see a man who told me everything I have ever done! He cannot be the Messiah, can he?" They left the city and were on their way to him.

—JOHN 4:16–30 NRSV

Many Samaritans from that city believed in him because of the woman's testimony, "He told me everything I have ever done." So when the Samaritans came to him, they asked him to stay with them; and he stayed there two days. And many more believed because of his word.

—JOHN 4:39–41 NRSV

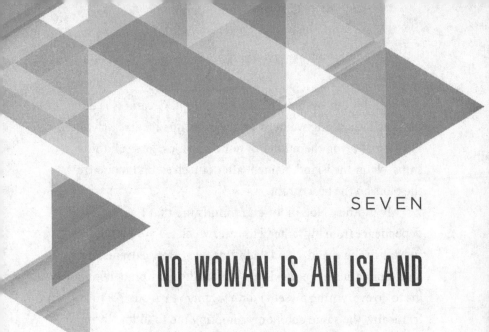

SEVEN

NO WOMAN IS AN ISLAND

Alone we can do so little; together
we can do so much.

—HELEN KELLER

I want to live as fiercely independently as possible.

It could be tempting to excuse my admission as just the way I am wired. Although, when it comes to self-reliance, my cabling is made of steel. What I am slow to admit is that self-sufficiency is not the way of Christ. Like any good girl raised to earn an honest living, I like getting what I deserve. Combine that rearing with living in a society that rewards the rene-gade bootstrappers living the American dream, and you've got a Christ follower who's supposed to rely upon the Lord with desperate dependence but who is keen on disproving "no woman is an island." Things have changed now post-internet.

The world is our oyster. The sky is the limit. Greatness is our destiny. Everything we need and want is one life hack away. Forget just being the master of our own ships; let's sail those ships, claim the island, name it after ourselves, and monetize the plots on the beachfront.

My mother, Noemi, often reminds me that I get my independence from my father. His case, which led to a lifetime of substance abuse and suicidal ideation, was more extreme, but his example helped me bridle the stampede in my brain telling me to do everything myself. I didn't want to turn out like him. Ironically, the same autonomy tempting me to follow in my father's footsteps was trying to convince me that if I tried hard enough, I could chart my own course and control all the outcomes. Apparently, self-sufficiency's cousin is self-deception.

Fear was my main motivator. Fear that history would repeat itself. Fear that my dad's problems were inescapable. When push came to shove, I was going to do what I needed to do *to survive*. Some of you know the destabilizing force involved when a parent is an addict. You learn early to fend for yourself. This is not to say I grew up feeling unloved, or that my upbringing involved hardships like poverty or abuse. My dad did the best he could and loved me dearly. I was never oppressed. But I often felt distressed. To cope, I tried to do life on my own.

Everything changed in college when my friend Becky invited me to join her small-group Bible study during summer break. At first I refused, citing the fact that people who "study" the Bible were strange. But thankfully, she was persistent. She couldn't wait to share her friends and her Jesus with me. At the time, I was eighteen years old and had been a Christian for only two years.

Hesitant and suspicious, I finally surrendered after she showed up at my house unannounced to make the ask face-to-face. How could I refuse her? She'd made the ultimate sacrifice: fighting Houston traffic to drive across the city to pick me up. That's what Houstonians call true love.

Becky was right, of course. I needed the group to learn how to love God and love others, lessons I could understand only in the context of community. There it was safe to ask questions and struggle with the mysteries of God. It would be a few more years before I would understand that the Christian God is tri-une. God is one essence and three distinct persons: Father, Son, and Holy Spirit. Three in one. God himself is proof that we need each other. Who better to live independently than a holy God? Yet he's in community with himself.

Becky couldn't wait for me to meet Kari, the Bible study's leader, an energetic and compassionate junior at Texas A&M University, where I was a freshman. Kari swept me up into her life and spent the next few years discipling me. Call it sisterhood, fellowship, family, tribe; call it whatever you want. I found people to live life with together. When my therapist asks me how I survived my college years without partying, I tell her about this small group of women who invited me into their love. They were the big sisters I didn't know I needed. Metaphorically speaking, they were the hands and feet of Jesus.

For a few years Kari and I met one-on-one for discipleship. I think Kari must have heard a sermon about finding the person in your circle of influence who knows the least about the

Bible but who is the most willing to learn, and then meeting with that person on a regular basis to talk about faith. By my own estimation, I happened to be the person in her life with the most biblical illiteracy and eagerness to learn about the Bible. So she put her faith into action. I remember Kari teaching me how to do a word study, character study, and book study in the Bible. To me her prayers sounded like music. I remember she was a great listener and made me feel loved, no matter what. At the time, Kari knew everything I had ever done, and she was well acquainted with my survival skills. She was trying to teach me a new way to live in Christ—to enjoy fellowship with God and with others. It was the purest form of life-on-life discipleship and my first introduction to spiritual big sistering.

Twenty years as a Christian has taught me that following Jesus means abandoning our own way. If I'm honest, I don't naturally like the fact that surrendering is required to follow in Jesus' footsteps. But I have come to love it, even glory in it. Jesus had to show me how everything I was doing to survive was actually keeping me from living life to the fullest. He did the same thing with the woman at the well in John 4.

As Jesus' conversation with the Samaritan woman progressed, he asked her to go and call her husband and come back with the man in tow. It was a request Jesus knew she couldn't manage. Her response was truthful; she didn't have a husband. Thanks to the historical-context study of great Bible scholars, we see that her circumstances were not a result of rebelliousness. In fact, as I'll explain below, she was just trying to survive. Jesus affirmed her truth telling with this statement: "You have had five husbands, and the one you have now is not your husband" (v. 17 NRSV). What I hope we will see together in this woman's story is that none of us can thrive in life independently. And unless our survival techniques include surrendering to Jesus, we will hitch ourselves to people and provisions that won't meet our deepest needs.

HARLOT TO HARD KNOCKS

All my life I've been taught that the woman at the well was a harlot. The picture painted for me at church was of a scantily dressed, salty-mouthed temptress who lured men with her wiles and then bounced as soon as she tired of their company. Her life was used to illustrate why we shouldn't divorce, why sex outside marriage is wrong, and how Jesus is going to call out promiscuity when he finds out how naughty we are. Want to know why this dejected woman was alone at the well, ashamed of her life? She was loose. Or so I used to think. What else could explain five marriages and a live-in boyfriend?

I'm indebted to the work of two amazing Bible scholars on this chapter of the Bible, and I want to mention them up front and attribute all of what I say next to the influence of either Dr. Lynn Cohick, provost and dean at Denver Seminary, or Dr. Norfleete Day, who before retiring was part of the Beeson Divinity School faculty at Samford University. Neither woman is an outlier in her interpretations. In fact, a significant number of scholars over the centuries have doubted the woman at the well was simply an uncommitted spouse. Instead, they say she was desperate to survive in a time when women were able to do that only with a man's help. To survive meant being tied to a man for provision and protection. To understand her predicament, we need to peek through a window into marriage in the ancient world.

According to Dr. Cohick, "most people in the ancient world got married—women most often in their teens, men in their late twenties."[1] If the woman at the well had been married five times and was on her sixth relationship, she must have been advanced in age, something that created even more vulnerability for women, since they were valued only as much as they were able to bear children. "Given the high death rate, people were often widowed and then remarried, perhaps two or three times."[2] So while we may frown upon or even judge someone who's been married several times, in the ancient world, and for the ancient reader of John 4, the Samaritan woman's multiple marriages were not shocking.

I love the way Dr. Cohick put it in her chapter in *Vindicating the Vixens*: "It's unlikely that she was divorced five times, each time committing adultery. No man in their right mind would marry a serial adulterer without money or fame. That she was a serial divorcee is also unlikely. She would have needed repeat male advocates to do so."[3]

Simply put, when the woman at the well agreed with Jesus that she had had five husbands and the one she was with was not her husband, it sounds like she was confessing sexual immorality. It sounds as though she had treated marriage flippantly in the past and was later cohabitating. But our assumption clashes with what we know to be true from history.

Dr. Cohick adds, "It's more likely that her five marriages and current arrangement were a result of unfortunate events that took the lives of several of her husbands."[4] Whatever the case, she was not presented in the text as a cheater but was depicted as a woman who'd suffered more than most. Best-case scenario for her latest relationship was that the man she was living with took pity on her old age and agreed to take her on as a second wife or concubine to make sure her physical needs were met.

As I walk alongside some of my dearest, most treasured soul friends, I can say with conviction that the loss suffered through divorce, no matter the reason, and the loss suffered through infertility, no matter the reason, have the power to kill joy, steal peace, and destroy future happiness. Reckoning with the aftermath of war, premature death, child loss, and general self-worth issues must have been a harrowing existence for the woman at the well. Using descriptions like *depressing*, *defeating*, *unbearable*, and *trauma*, my friends would tell you these in-between places in their lives felt like Shechem. All these years I've been reading into the Scriptures what I wanted or needed to see rather than seeing what could be the true circumstances of this woman's experience. How quickly I was able to write off the Samaritan woman's lifestyle without any time required to understand her plight.

Dr. Norfleete Day wrote the best book I've read on the woman at the well. It was her thesis back in the day. Now retired from Beeson Divinity School, Dr. Day asked, "Based on our knowledge of the social and cultural values of first-century Palestine, why would it be unnatural to assume that this woman deserves our sympathy rather than our judgment? In a society that granted women essentially no social or legal standing apart from a responsible father, man, husband, brother, or son, she can legitimately be considered a marginalized figure, subject to economic, social, and legal exploitation."[5] Five marriages indicated that this woman's life had been especially difficult.

Would you also describe your life as "especially difficult"? I will never understand why evil hounds some of us. Unfortunately, I've been in church long enough to know that sometimes when bad things happen to good people, we question their faith, their morality, and their commitment to Jesus. We don't slow down to try to walk a mile in someone's shoes before we declare with self-righteousness that they got themselves into this mess. Worse yet, sometimes we abandon people to their circumstances in the name of teaching them about consequences. They made their bed, and now they can lie in it. Here in John 4, I had done just that.

To again quote Dr. Day, if the woman at the well had five broken marriages that all ended in tragedy, and she was advanced in age and without means to support herself, "having a man to provide for her may have been her only means of survival in a cultural system that made no provision for independent women."[6]

Greta Gerwig, director of the most recent remake of the movie *Little Women*, has all my respect. I've been enjoying *Little Women* for years—when I was young through the book by Louisa May Alcott and later through Gillian Armstrong's adaptation in the 1994 movie with Winona Ryder. But I've never liked Amy's character. In Greta Gerwig's 2019 movie, she found a way to endear Amy to me. There's a scene in the movie where Amy tries to explain to her true love, Laurie, why she is willing to marry for money. With force, Amy says, "Don't sit there and tell me that marriage isn't an economic proposition, because it is."[7] Amy articulates, to a lesser degree, what the woman at the well had lived through five times. Amy's survival, and the survival of her family, all depended upon her marrying a wealthy man.

Sometimes when we are trying our darndest to get out of our stuckness, to get out of the tight squeeze between a rock and a hard place, all of our choices feel impossible. To anyone feeling regret over choices you've made in your in-between places, choices you never would have made otherwise, let the shame go. Forget what others think about you and any resulting outcome of those choices. There is at least one person who's lived through worse. He sees all your pain and the circumstances surrounding your choices. His name is Jesus. He makes no false assumptions about you; he doesn't slander or gossip about you. But he also doesn't look the other way when your feeble attempts to stay alive are actually threatening your faith. I don't fault the woman at the well for doing what she had to do to stay alive. But I'm so thankful Jesus showed her how to truly live.

I wonder if Jesus was making a point here: the woman's obvious need was for food, water, and shelter, but she also lacked the fulfillment of her deepest emotional needs. To be seen, understood, listened to, valued, protected, and loved. What if Jesus' statements about her marriages and living arrangement were not indictments? What if they accurately represented her as a victim of a system that depersonalized her? What if Jesus wasn't just teaching her a theological lesson that she was ready to hear and willing to accept, and that she eventually used to win others for Christ; what if he was also expressing his compassion and concern for the suffering she had endured and the hardships she had experienced? Wouldn't this make sense for a woman in a place like Shechem? It's highly likely that instead of being promiscuous, she had just suffered a lot of really hard knocks, and to survive she needed the protection of a man in her life. Her previous husbands and her current live-in companion may have been covering her survival needs, but none of them could meet her deepest need for a Savior—the kind of Savior who comes to us in our most broken, tension-filled in-between places.

Why was this woman married five times and living with someone not her husband? To survive. *To live.* Who better to talk to her about living water than the author of her existence? He's the only one who could truly sustain her and quench her thirst for independence.

When Jesus said, "Go and call your husband," is it possible she understood his meaning to be, *I know how hard life has been for you*? When she answered him with the statement that she was not married, is it possible that was another way of saying, *This was the only way I could survive; this is the only way to carry on*? When Jesus said, "You've been married five times, and the man you live with now is not your husband," do you think she understood his meaning to be, *The hard knocks you've weathered didn't escape my view. I see all your pain*?

I'd never suggest to add words to the Bible. What I will offer is a way to read the words she said to the townspeople who heard her testimony. She said, "He told me everything I did." I wonder if they would have understood her meaning the way I understand it. Jesus had told her everything she had done *to survive*. He'd told her everything she'd done *to live*. He had uncovered her deepest fear: that all the men she'd looked to to save her could not. I wonder if marriage represented an in-between place to her.

What if God brought to our attention everything we've done to get through this life? Would a conversation with him reveal we've been looking for help in all the wrong places? What would Jesus say to you if he were to bring to your attention your greatest need or desire? Would it be something you are proud of or something that grosses you out? Here's my reminder to you, as I speak it to myself in the mirror: no woman is an island, and no existence is really living without Jesus as the provider of all our needs.

If you and I were peering over our steaming cups of tea or coffee while discussing this part of the woman at the well's story, I'd lean in and ask you what survival skills you've been trying to master and if they are serving you well. Is your survival tactic perfectionism? Our in-between places are fertile ground for the seeds of "If I can just get this perfect, I'll move forward." Is your survival tactic apathy? Are you choosing not to care or numbing yourself from excitement by choosing not to celebrate your wins? Focusing on our own potential seems to be another popular survival tactic many of us venture into when we feel lost or stuck. Or maybe your survival tactic is isolation—hiding yourself away from your friends, declining get-togethers, opting out of Bible study and small group, rejecting invitations to get out of the house. None of these tactics will make your in-between place less Shechem-like. In fact, I think they will make it worse.

Grasping at perfection, apathy, and isolation won't serve you well in the long run. I know you know that already, so give them up. Give up on survival tactics and give in to Jesus' sufficiency, vision, and companionship.

THE BUDDY SYSTEM WORKS

Kari and I hadn't seen each other for many years until we shared a stage at a conference in College Station, Texas, home of the fightin' Texas Aggies (*whoop*). Backstage I was dying to ask her some reflective questions. Now that I was running an organization that disciples young women, I wanted to know her secrets of mentoring success. If I could find a way to replicate my college discipleship experience with Kari and pass it on to others, it would be a huge win for Polished.

To my shock, none of my questions got the answers I expected. When I asked Kari what curriculum she used when we met together, she laughed. There was no study guide, she swore. I told her that couldn't be right because I always remember her having something Bible-ish to say to me. She laughed again the way people laugh when they hear something ridiculous. Kari said she would pray before we met and ask God to help her listen well and encourage me with anything she'd heard recently at church. All I can say is that she was really good at recycling the messages of the sermons she was listening to, because Kari was a walking Bible dictionary.

When I asked her how she planned the agenda for our time together, she grabbed my arm and brought me in close for a big hug. She joked that I was so silly. There was never an agenda or a plan.

"Are you kidding with me? I'm genuinely asking, Kari!" I responded. Our time together felt like it was all predetermined and moving with purpose in a clear direction of under-standing. Kindly she assured me that if there was anything accomplished during discipleship meetings, it was because the presence of God showed up.

All this time I was concerned about methods and lesson planning, when Kari's effectiveness didn't have a lick to do with either. Yes, she was a diligent student of the Scriptures and a faithful witness of God's power. But she said something profound to me when I asked her the secret. She said, "Kat, I think the secret was that we were doing it together. We had each other." As usual, there was Kari with the mic drop.

Kari means so much to me. After all, because of her bid-ding I became the chaplain of our sorority my junior year in college, against my better judgment. Kari asked me to run for office, which I never would have done without her years of investment in me. I think my exact response to Kari's sugges-tion that I succeed her as chaplain was "Are you nuts?" She likely doesn't remember persuading me to run for the office, but I remember. She said something to the effect of "It's time to pass on what you've learned. Like a cup overflowing, just let the Spirit spill over into somebody else's life." If asked why I love teaching the Bible, the answer would be because of the time I spent serving as chaplain of Sigma Phi Lambda.

It's laughable to think I've somehow overcome my desire for fierce independence. I still fight those tendencies daily. I'll tell you this, though. I know there's something better than secluding myself on an island. I know what it is, in small part and with feeble attempts, to be planted next to streams of living water. Lessons are learned in communion with God and his people while we study the Scriptures together.

I share all this with you because there are some parallels with my own experience and the woman at the well's. You see, after she learned that Jesus was the man she'd needed all her life, she ran with the gospel news and shared it with others. She didn't keep it to herself or for herself; she testified.

In the next chapter we'll see she was brave enough to accept truth and live accordingly. May we all follow in her footsteps.

Discussion Questions

1. Do you struggle with independence or codependence? If so, when do you think that started?
2. How would your life be different if you shed those survival skills for dependence upon Christ?
3. What is a tangible way you could resist independence or codependence and opt for dependence upon Christ?
4. Describe a time when you felt misunderstood for your choices.

5. How could the church do a better job of supporting people through a divorce?
6. Is anyone mentoring you? What do you love most about their mentorship?

Study Guide

Visit www.katarmstrong.com/theinbetweenplace to download the free study guide. Materials for chapter 7 include

- a link to Dr. Norfleete Day's thesis
- a podcast about life after divorce

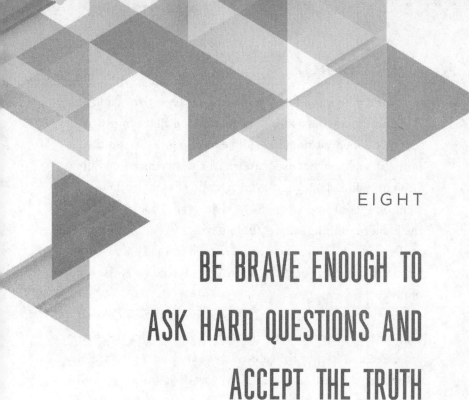

EIGHT

BE BRAVE ENOUGH TO ASK HARD QUESTIONS AND ACCEPT THE TRUTH

There is no magic in small plans. When I consider
my ministry, I think of the world. Anything less
than that would not be worthy of Christ.

—HENRIETTA MEARS

Combine the global influence of Young Life Ministries, CRU
(the name for Campus Crusade for Christ in the United
States), Navigators, and the ministry of Billy Graham, and
you'll have a fraction of the impact Henrietta Mears had on

133

our world. She was a force. Henrietta has been referred to as the "grandmother of us all."[1] The founders of all the ministries just mentioned sat under her Bible teaching or shaped their ministries around her expertise on Christian education. Billy Graham, Bill Bright, Jim Rayburn, and Dawson Trotman all went on record to give credit to Henrietta at some point in their tenure running some of the largest evangelistic ministries in the world. If I had a short list of women from history whom I could invite over for dinner, Henrietta would be at the top of my list.

She started her career as a Bible teacher at just eleven years old; her first class was at a Minneapolis mission for the marginalized and impoverished. Just six years later, at the age of seventeen, she dedicated her life to vocational ministry with plans to be a missionary to China. (I nod to all the women reading this book who at one point thought God was calling them to be a missionary overseas.) Instead, Henrietta served as a missionary every place she lived in the United States.

As I studied her life, I saw a pattern emerge. With every move to a new city, every new post in a leadership position, she gathered a handful of Bible students and grew ministries that defied the odds. One of her classes for young women at First Baptist Minneapolis grew to three thousand by the end of her ten years teaching the class. By all measures, her Sunday school class outnumbered many megachurches. In 1928, she started a thirty-five-year tenure as the director of Christian education at a Presbyterian church in Hollywood, California. She grew Sunday school attendance from 450 students to 6,500 students. *What?*

But that doesn't include the thousands of people she led to Christ one-on-one. In addition to innovating the modern-day Sunday school movement, perfecting the model, and replicating it around the world, she found time to meet with thousands of people she would then convert to Christ. Talk about a disciple maker. She made not only disciples of Jesus but also disciple-making disciples who now reach billions of people worldwide. Her MO was to find gaps in young people's training for understanding the Scriptures, then create systems and curriculum to bridge the gaps. When something just wouldn't do, she'd fix it. Unimpressed with the Sunday school material being offered to students, she ended up writing her own. *Of course she did.* And then she started her own publishing company to reproduce her new material. I love her so much, it's not even funny.

Richard J. Leyda serves as associate professor of Christian education and chair of the Christian education department at Talbot School of Theology, Biola University. In an article about Henrietta's influence on Christian education, he wrote, "Surveying the Sunday school materials currently being used as well as curriculum from other publishers, she found that nothing was adequate to meet the needs of students." The publishing company met the national demand for her work, and her "publications were known for their quality, student appeal, and emphasis on life application. They were biblically focused and Christ-centered, yet also took into account current educational understanding about how students best learned."[2]

I don't think the phrase *thought-leader* existed in her time, but she certainly was one. That characteristic naturally led her to become the cofounder of the National Sunday School Association. You see, finding the problem, creating the solution, and reproducing effective tools wasn't enough for Henrietta. National training needed to be offered so her methods could accompany her writings. While most overlooked the education of young adults and children, she believed young people were going to change the world for Jesus and needed to be equipped for the gospel work. Well respected and even revered by her peers, she operated as an equal with the pastors she served under to grow their churches and ministries. She had zero patience for the folks getting in the way of her mission work, but she didn't bulldoze over anybody.

To trail-blaze, Henrietta must have been asking deep theological questions. What methods and materials work best for young students of the Bible? How do we win more people to Jesus? How do we replicate successful strategies and share best practices with teachers around the nation? She must have studied the Scriptures and her students with inquisitive devotion. I wonder if other Christian educators have pondered the same questions with the same tenacity. Seems to me, Henrietta was asking hard questions and wouldn't be satisfied until she found the answers.

Henrietta is described as an "anomaly" and "a woman far ahead of her time."[3] These are two descriptions I might apply to the woman at the well too. The Samaritan woman asked deep theological questions of Jesus during their conversation and revealed that she anticipated a Messiah was coming. Jesus revealed himself to her as "I am," something he'd never done before (John 4:26). John 4 serves as a reminder that Jesus entrusts women with theological training just as he does men, and he intends for us to use that training to lead and love others. Anything less is a departure from God's design. Like the woman at the well, Henrietta Mears used her testimony to win others for Christ in her community. We don't know the names of the men and women living in Shechem who came to faith in Christ because of the Samaritan woman's faithful witness, but I wonder if some of them went on to build the kingdom with passions similar to those of Billy Graham, Bill Bright, Jim Rayburn, Dawson Trotman, or Henrietta Mears.

LOCATION, LOCATION, LOCATION

One of the burning questions the woman at the well asked Jesus was about where to worship God. Why did she care so much about this? Was her question simply a diversion tactic? I don't think so. Realtors are not the only ones who champion location, location, location. When one's religious practice must take place in a temple in order to be in relationship with God, every religious person cares about where the temple is located. The Samaritan woman was simply asking the most important theological question of her day: Where can I worship God?

As Christ followers, we can worship and connect with God anywhere—inside a church building, in our homes, or even in our cars. In fact, three of my favorite times connecting with God have not been on a Sunday morning in a church building. Topping my list would be worshiping God on a farm in Shelby Farms, Tennessee, while the rain was pouring down on my poncho at a conference called OneDay.[4] Another would be on a beach in Costa Rica while a pink sunset melted into the blue ocean waves, and another was in the Colorado Rocky Mountains in a horse stable huddled around some of my nearest and dearest girlfriends at a retreat called Camp Well.

We can offer God our praises and devotion at any time in any place because, according to 1 Corinthians 3:16, if we are in relationship with Christ, our bodies have become God's temple through the indwelling presence of the Holy Spirit. Not so for the believers living during the Samaritan woman's lifetime. Staying connected to God during her day meant offering praise and sacrifices in the temple. The difficulty she faced was trying to figure out which temple was the right one, because both the Jews and the Samaritans had temples to worship God.

The Jewish temple was located in Jerusalem, and the Samaritans' was on Mount Gerizim, just up the hill from the in-between place where Jesus and the woman were having their conversation. Part of the animosity between Jews and Samaritans was about forbidden access to the inner courts of each other's temples and the offerings acceptable from either group.

We have friends who are members of other churches who regularly drop into our Sunday services at Dallas Bible Church for various reasons, and it's never an issue for anyone. We are delighted to welcome anyone who comes to Dallas Bible. Not so with the Jews and Samaritans fighting over whose temple was the true temple. The Jews treated Samaritans like they were outsiders to God's fellowship, so they didn't have access to the inner parts of the temple and couldn't participate in the same way as the Jews. Imagine my husband, Aaron, lead pastor at our church, telling our friends visiting on a Sunday morning that they could enter the building but not go into the sanctuary. Or that they could listen to the message at the coffee station but not make an offering when the plates were passed.

Samaritans and Jews held in common a strong mono-theistic faith in the God of Abraham, Isaac, and Jacob. What divided the two ethnic groups was the Samaritans' insistence that Mount Gerizim was the holy place for sacrifice, and Moses was the Messiah. Jews believed Jerusalem was the holy place for sacrifice, and that a Messiah would come after Moses. The Samaritans' reasoning was logical, although it was wrong. Mount Gerizim was the location of Abel's altar (Gen. 4:4), the site of Noah's sacrifice after the flood (Gen. 8:20), the meeting place of Abraham and Melchizedek (Gen. 14:17–18), and the site of Isaac's intended sacrifice (Gen. 22), to name a few important events.[5] Since Samaritans believed only the first five biblical books of the Old Testament scriptures to be inspired, Moses became the future Messiah (Deut. 18:15–18). Moses was considered not only the chief prophet but also "the light of the world."[6] Samaritans believed Moses would return and restore worship to the proper mountain, Mount Gerizim, proving the Samaritans were right and the Jews were wrong. Why was the woman at the well asking Jesus about where to worship God? Because Jesus had just proved he was a prophet by pointing out all she'd been doing to survive, she believed his answer would determine who was right about the Messiah.

Like any religious Samaritan, the woman at the well anticipated Moses would come back and prove the temple belonged on Mount Gerizim, but she knew there were arguments between her people and the Jews about who was right about the prophecies describing a Messiah. What I find fascinating is that right after the moment she realized she was talking to a prophet, someone who knew about her struggle to survive without any mention from her, she asked Jesus to confirm or deny her faith. Think about the implications of his answer: he would affirm that worship was supposed to be either on Mount Gerizim or in Jerusalem. His correction would have a profound destabilizing effect on the only faith she'd ever known. She asked anyway. She had the guts to ask a deep, hard question that would determine how she worshiped God and whether she was worshiping the one true God or a fake.

Jesus did not rebuke her for trying to skirt the subject of her living arrangements or her last five marriages. No. He not only entertained her question but also took the time to answer it and teach her doctrines of the faith that none had heard yet. Jesus would tell her that a time was coming when there would no longer be any division between Jews and Samaritans. Not only was Jerusalem the right answer for temple worship, but soon, he said, a time would come when the temple location would not be the deciding factor in someone's faith. Jesus explained that *how*, not *where*, someone approached God would be the litmus test for true faith. He said it this way: "True worshipers will worship the Father in spirit and truth" (John 4:23 NRSV).

The phrase "in Spirit and truth" is a figure of speech similar to the phrase "shock and awe." Former Dallas Theological Seminary professor and Bible exposition department head Dr. Thomas L. Constable explained that Jesus was expressing "a single complex idea" with two components. He suggested translating the phrase "in spirit and in truth" as "truly spiritual."[7] The woman at the well was the first person Jesus entrusted with this theology lesson.

This part of their conversation points to another in-between place. The woman had lived her whole life one way, and with a few sentences from Jesus, her whole paradigm shifted, but she would continue to live, for a while, in an in-between time, before truly spiritual worship replaced temple worship. And this shift was not just for this woman or the other Samaritans who would come to faith in Christ. It would mean the Jews would have to alter the way they worshiped God as well. Although Jerusalem was the proper home for the temple, soon the temple would be obsolete.

The author of Hebrews used his entire book in the New Testament to help Jewish Christians sort out this disorienting truth: Jesus is the new and better High Priest. Through Jesus' life, death, and resurrection, the ways Jews used to be in communion with God no longer applied. The implications were astounding. Most of life for first-century Jews revolved around a religious calendar devoted to honoring religious feasts and festivals all taking place at the temple. Everyone would have been familiar with—tied to, even—the sacrificial system requiring the purchase of animals and food to offer at the temple. Jesus changed everything. Priests were no longer needed; Jesus fulfilled that position. Sacrifices were no longer needed; Jesus fulfilled that requirement. And the temple was no longer needed; Jesus fills our lives with his presence and makes our bodies the new temple. The author of Hebrews wrote that our response to Jesus bringing heaven to earth is to draw near to him with a "true heart in full assurance of faith, with our hearts sprinkled clean from an evil conscience and our bodies washed in pure water" (10:22).

As difficult as it may have been to accept Jesus' words, the woman at the well seems to have taken them in with readiness. Emboldened by all the truth Jesus entrusted to her, she brought the good news of a new way of worship to a group of people convinced otherwise. And they believed her!

You know what she said in response to Jesus' Bible lesson? She said she *knew* the Messiah was coming, and when he did he would explain everything. This reminds me of the kinds of questions I ask my son: "I *know* you're going to clean up your room before you take a bath, right?" The woman did the opposite. She used a statement to ask the question, "Are you the Messiah?" If Jesus was going to disclose his divinity, now was a prime opportunity. Jesus responded by saying, "I am he, the one who is speaking to you" (John 4:26 NRSV).

For years I've interpreted the woman at the well's question about where to worship God as an attempt to detour the conversation, but it turns out she was just a deep thinker. She wasn't on a rabbit trail; she was digging a well with her words. She was a hard-question asker. She was *brave*. She was courageous enough to ask a question all of her peers assumed they knew the right answer to. She spoke up anyway.

ASK ANYWAY

Taylor Nichols and I met during a mountaintop experience. We were both attending Camp Well, a gathering for doers and dreamers, when our hearts were united around a desire to help women explore their faith. She has a God-given gift for holding space for Christians wrestling with doubt. Overchurched and dechurched wanderers find their way to Taylor, and she's their gentle guide to the truth about Jesus and his way. Taylor's the kind of friend who texts you thirty minutes before your big event to ask if there is anything you forgot to pick up so she can take care of it for you. She's the kind of friend who won't allow shame to take root in your thoughts or words. If she hears you start to describe yourself in negative ways, she will stop you midsentence with a palm in the air. Taylor's the kind of friend who invites you to be your most authentic self, all judgments aside, and then gets to the heart of the matter weighing you down.

When she asked me to be on her podcast, *Speak Life*, I knew she would ask me about my father's suicide, because she's one of the rare women in my life who asks me really hard questions and can handle the tension in my answers. Guided by the Holy Spirit, she's wise enough to help you know when you are oversharing but bold enough to challenge you to be honest with yourself and with others. You know you are safe with Taylor. To date, my podcast episode with her is the most vulnerable I've been in talking about my father's passing. Her podcast is not like Oprah's famed couch, where people used to go to divulge secrets for high-ratings entertainment. Confiding in Taylor isn't for sport. She really wants to know truth, which is Jesus, and to understand your truth, your experience.

I've shared with you that one of my most treasured worship experiences was in a horse stable in the Colorado Rocky Mountains. Guess who I was seated next to? Taylor Nichols. She knows I'm a city girl through and through, so she made sure to make fun of the fact that I was surrounded by farm animals and it was so cold I could see my breath. There's no one I'd rather freeze my heinie off with than Taylor.

Last week she texted me while I was in the middle of writing this book. She said she was a little embarrassed to ask me some questions about the Bible, but she just had to know more about what she was reading in her Bible study. A small group of women were headed to her house, and in her preparation time, she found a gap in her own understanding of the Scriptures. She described the feeling in the pit in her stomach that we all feel when we think we should know the answer to something and feel dumb for even bringing it up. You know what I'm talking about? Seems like everyone else passed the basics of Christianity, and somehow you failed to grasp the fundamentals. Like raising your hand in class only to find out that if you had read the syllabus, the professor wouldn't have had to repeat his instructions. Thing is, Taylor Nichols never asks dumb questions. And neither do you. How on earth are we supposed to learn if we can't explore?

Want to know her theology question? Taylor was wrestling with predestination, that God has foreknowledge about our coming to faith in Christ; and free will, that we make our own choices in life. Now it was my turn to poke at Taylor the way she did in that stable many years ago. I joked that her curiosity was not level 101. There's nothing basic about sorting out how two seemingly incompatible truths coexist in a way we can't understand this side of heaven. People spend their whole lives trying to work out the answers to those most existential questions of the Christian faith. Leave it to Taylor to ask penetrating, crucial questions. She reminds me of the woman at the well and Henrietta Mears.

I want us to be more like all three of the women I've described to you. Maybe you need to emulate Taylor Nichols and start asking more questions about Jesus and the Bible, even if you feel stupid doing so. We need Taylor's chutzpah. Isn't God worth our momentary feelings of insecurity for a lifetime of confidence in Christ? If you find yourself starting questions with the disclaimer, "This might be a stupid question, but . . ." take a second and shake off the Enemy's super-effective tactic of keeping us tied to confusion or disillusion or pride. Ask anyway. Raise your hand and get the answers. I think it's Taylor's commitment to holding space in tension-filled in-between places that helps her press into hard conversations and raise her hand for insight. She's used to being brave, and I'm praying you and I will be as well. We might not discover all the answers we're looking for, but our doubts will lessen as our capacity to accept mystery increases.

Maybe you're ready to be more like Henrietta Mears. Maybe you've asked a lot of questions of the Bible and found life-changing answers. Now it's time for you to find the gaps in someone else's understanding and share your findings. Who knows, maybe you are supposed to write curriculum for your church or cofound an organization that meets the needs of Bible students. Maybe you are the trailblazer a future Billy Graham needs to learn from. I would imagine that Henrietta was always coming against the inhibitors of innovation: fear and self-doubt. She plowed forward anyway. When I consider what it must have been like to sit in her pastoral staff meetings and ask why things were being done in a certain way, I laugh. What a sight it must have been to see her challenge the status quo, to cast a vision for something never done before, and to commit to the grueling, all-consuming work needed to do something new.

Or maybe you need to be more like the woman at the well. If Jesus were standing right in front of you, what question would you ask him about your faith practice? Why not devote time to researching that subject? You could make an appointment with your pastor or spiritual mentor and ask for guidance and direction. If you feel uneasy about your questions or what to do with the answers once you find them, you're in good company. The Samaritan woman risked a whole paradigm shift for truth. And her faithful witness involved asking one feeble question to the townspeople she wanted to convert: "He cannot be the Messiah, can he?" (John 4:29 NRSV). Her mission work boiled down to asking a question she was still wrestling with herself. By putting herself out there to Jesus and her community, she joined an exclusive list of pioneering women of the Bible. As the first person to hear Jesus disclose he was Messiah and the first evangelist, she secured her spot on the "She's the First" list I've got in my office, which includes women like Hagar, the first to name God; Lydia, the first Christian in Europe; Mary of Nazareth, the first disciple of Jesus; and Mary Magdalene, the first gospel preacher. Go ahead. Ask the hard questions. And then ready yourself for a paradigm shift.

Discussion Questions

1. Describe the most worshipful experience you've ever had. Where did it take place?
2. Why do you think your connection with God was so strong?
3. If you could have dinner with three women from Christian history, who would be on your list?
4. Who are the trailblazing women of faith in your life?
5. Name one hard question about your faith you wish you knew the answer to.
6. Do you come to the Bible to help you find answers? Why or why not?

Study Guide

Visit www.katarmstrong.com/theinbetweenplace to download the free study guide. Materials for chapter 8 include

- a link to the *Speak Life* podcast
- a picture of Kat and Taylor at Camp Well
- a link to Camp Well retreats
- an article about the Samaritan belief system

NINE

DROP YOUR DISTRACTIONS

Have guts enough to choose the
things that matter now.

—BETH MOORE

Aaron knows the way to earn his brownie points: buy me movie tickets to a film with a strong female lead. If there's a new release in the theaters celebrating women, he's wise enough to take me on opening weekend. The movies never live up to the history books, in my humble opinion, but they have the power to bring to life dimensions of stories otherwise lost on a page in a book or in an audio recording.

On this particular date night, we saw *Harriet*, the movie about Harriet Tubman, the freedom-fighting, army-leading, Underground Railroad–conducting force of liberation. Risking her life and defying the odds, she escaped her slave owners and fled more than one hundred miles on foot, by herself, to freedom. Her journey from Maryland to Philadelphia almost killed her, but she lived to see her promised land. Harriet was born Araminta Ross, until she changed her name to Harriet Tubman in honor of her mother. The name change commemorated her new life as a free woman.

Her harrowing journey through the Underground Railroad, a network that helped smuggle slaves into Union territory, enabled her to scout the routes she would later use to help others escape the evils of slavery. According to PBS, she made nineteen trips into the South and escorted more than three hundred slaves to freedom over the course of a decade. She would boast that she "never lost a single passenger."[1] Harriet Tubman has no rival; she was the most effective conductor of the Underground Railroad. Astounded by her tenacity and urgency, her friends and supporters tried everything in their power to persuade her to remain in safety and enjoy her freedom, but her conscience wouldn't allow her to leave her loved ones in harm's way. She would help others to freedom or die. Her unrelenting passion and fortitude shocked even the most committed abolitionists, as she would often challenge influential freedom fighters to solidarity to the cause. And she could do so with authority because she was willing to put her own life on the line for the antislavery movement. Although some tried to reason some restraint into her, she wouldn't be controlled ever again. Not by a slave owner, not by a Confederate South, and certainly not by the free people hoping to win the Civil War. Harriet charted her own course, and no one could argue with her success rate or her integrity.

Harriet was a devoted Christian woman who lived out her faith with reckless abandon to Jesus. The movie about her life, which was released in 2019, featured several scenes that likely took some liberties to embody her spiritual fervor and Holy Spirit–led missions, but the movie does a great job presenting Harriet as a woman who believed she heard God's voice, and it was his presence that guided her on each of her nineteen trips into enemy territory. Nothing rattled her; she feared only God and chose to listen to his guidance even when his leading made no sense. She attributed her safety and that of her passengers to God's protection. Leading abolitionist John Brown wrote many letters that mentioned Harriet. He said she was one of the bravest people on the continent and even called her "General Tubman."[2]

After Harriet completed her last rescue mission, she served as a spy, scout, and leader in the Union army until the Civil War was over. According to the National Women's History Museum, Harriet was the first African American woman to serve in the military.[3]

Harriet's life reminds me of the woman at the well because both women were Moses figures in their stories. Review any history book or biography about Harriet Tubman, and you'll find that her most recognizable title is "the Moses of her people."[4] She liberated slaves in the same way Moses liberated the Israelites from Egyptian slavery. The uproar over Harriet's escape and the escape of all the slaves she was rescuing caused her former owners to hire bounty hunters and offer up a $40,000 reward for her capture.[5] Rumors swept the South that "Moses" was in their midst.

The woman at the well's encounter with her Savior has sacred echoes of Moses' burning-bush experience. Exploring the connection will enable us to move forward in confidence from our in-between places. When we read the stories of Moses and the woman at the well side by side, we see that both people were stuck in an in-between place where God set them free. Maybe the hardest part in our breaking free from stuckness is moving from doubt to faith, something both Moses and the woman at the well had to do.

The good news is that you and I don't need to wait on Moses or a Moses-type to be released from the gravitational pull of sin. We have Jesus.

As I sit and listen to women trudging through their in-between places in life, I just have to cry along with them. I, too, know how painful and frustrating it can be to feel directionless and unmotivated, and to wish for change. If you feel trapped in your in-between place, it might be that you are stuck in the bondage of sin. Not everyone fighting for hope while they wait on their future is in sin. Hear me, please. But maybe you need to be set free from the bondage of sin to experience forward motion in life. Hang with me here. Don't tune me out. You might need a burning-bush moment before you close this book if you really want God to change your story.

FIRE VERSUS WATER

Abraham, Jacob, and Joseph certainly have a place of prominence in Old Testament literature, but none compare to

Moses. Even his birth signals the miraculous ways God set apart his life. You can sense from his birth story that not even Pharaoh's edict to kill all the firstborn Hebrew baby boys could keep this special baby from fulfilling the calling on his life, a call to usher oppressed people into freedom. As Tremper Longman III and Raymond B. Dillard have rightly pointed out, the exodus story is one of the most foundational stories in all of the Old Testament, as it narrates the "paradigmatic salvation event of ancient Israel."[6] Simply put, the exodus story was God's greatest act of salvation in the Old Testament, and Moses was the leader of the movement. Yet his future success in leadership and providential upbringing did not exempt the most important Old Testament hero of the faith from the lurking darkness in his heart.

Moses was caught in a no-win situation as a young Hebrew man living as Egyptian royalty. Certainly he must have been confused about his own identity. He fit nowhere, really. My mouth fell open when I started researching Moses' story and reading Dr. Nyasha Junior's commentary on Moses' "in-betweenness." In the *Women's Bible Commentary*, she says Moses' ability to "pass" as an Egyptian to Zipporah and her sisters highlights "his in-betweenness in both the Israelite and Egyptian communities."[7] He'd lived a privileged life in Egypt as the adopted son of Pharaoh's daughter and must have been accustomed to seeing the ruthless injustice the Egyptian slave masters held over his people, the Hebrew slaves. One particular act of cruelty set him off. The darkness in his soul that would enable murder must have been eating him alive for many years. When he found an Egyptian beating a Hebrew man, Moses impulsively killed the abuser and buried him before fleeing the Egyptian palace to an in-between place— the desert of Midian. Midian was Moses' Samaria. In between a childhood in the Egyptian palace and the parting of the Red Sea, Moses lived in Midian.

We saw earlier that the first thing Moses did upon arriving in Midian was sit down next to a well (Ex. 2:15). *Hold up.* Since we know the whole Bible story and we know that Jesus, the greatest liberator, would make a trip to a certain well in John 4, we should start to connect the dots between the two stories. Wells could be considered origin symbols, the place where new life and sustained life happens. In Moses' story, he needed the living water, or God's presence, because he was about to face the fire, quite literally, in the form of a burning bush. Little did he know that the crucible of leadership would hold his feet to the fire on more than a few occasions. How did he survive the tests of his own faith and the grumbling tests of leading others into more faith? God's nearness.

Moses and the woman at the well share a lot in common— namely, lots of in-between experiences. Of utmost importance is that both Moses and the woman at the well experienced a theophany, an appearance of the Divine: she at the well and he at the burning bush. While Moses was shepherding a flock on Mount Horeb, an angel of the Lord appeared to him in a flame of fire within a bush (Ex. 3:2). Shockingly, the bush on fire was not consumed. Many now refer to Moses' experience as his burning-bush moment.

Both Moses' story and the woman at the well's prove, again, that some of our spiritual transformation is reserved for our in-between places. Those defining moments that rattle our confidence in God's timing or plan. Times in our lives when we wish we could turn back to the familiar. Seasons of our lives that we are ashamed to be stuck in. All these Samaria-like areas of our comings and goings on our journeys have purpose. Namely, they teach us more about who God is. Every time he will confirm that he is a loving Father working all things for our good.

I find it interesting that Moses' burning-bush moment and the Samaritan woman's living-water moment both have a backdrop of oppression. As Moses recorded his own history through Exodus 1, he was quick to remind his readers that a new generation of power ruled in Egypt, one that didn't remember Joseph, the Israelite who served the Egyptian pharaoh and ended up saving the whole country. That means the taskmasters oppressing the Hebrews through slavery in Moses' day didn't anticipate that God would rescue his people as he had done before through an unlikely liberator like Joseph. The favor God had upon Joseph's life to interpret Pharaoh's dreams secured not only his own freedom but the survival of all the people in Egypt and surrounding areas facing famine. Yet no one in leadership remembered this important bit of history when Moses was born.

God's people were crying out for his intervention in the exodus story. The woman at the well was a marginalized person herself and was likely also crying out to God to save her life.

Both Moses and the Samaritan woman probably struggled to cope with their identities apart from their biggest failures in life. Struggles everyone around them knew full well. I'm convinced both of them had come to the end of themselves. Moses was living on the other side of murder and cowardice, and she was surviving on the other side of abandonment, loss, and helplessness. Outcasts to their people, class, and society, and both humble seekers, they experienced a hope-filled encounter with God in their in-between places.

After marrying Zipporah, Moses became the shepherd of his father-in-law's flocks. One day Moses took the flocks to the far side of the wilderness in Midian, to the "mountain of God," or Mount Horeb, where the angel of the Lord appeared to him in the burning bush (Ex. 3). While Moses' encounter with the angel of the Lord was on top of a mountain, the woman at the well's encounter with Jesus happened next to a mountain and included a conversation about where to worship God. After God commissioned Moses to tell Pharaoh to let his people go, he told Moses that after they escaped, they would all worship on Mount Sinai together, which echoes the conversation Jesus had with the Samaritan woman about a time when people would gather together, not on a mountain, but in a truly spiritual way. Both mountaintop experiences yield new understandings of the one true God. He gathers his people and they worship him. Pharaoh or slavery or desperation cannot stand in the way of our Way Maker. And his presence is not constrained to one single place any more than we are constrained to stay in our in-between places forever. He will set us free.

Moses saw God as a flame in a burning bush, while the woman at the well had an in-depth conversation with Jesus as the living water. What piqued Moses' interest was the fact that the bush was not consumed by the fire. In the Samaritan woman's story, she couldn't believe there was a new kind of water, living water, that would never run dry. The fire-versus-water motif cannot be overlooked in a comparison of the narratives. As readers of both stories, we should see the impact God is creating through these beautiful echoes. Appear as he may through fire or water, God cannot be extinguished. But as our lives are consumed in his presence, the dross of sin melts away like gold purified in a fire, and the stickiness of desperation is washed away in his living water like residue being carried away in the bath.

When Moses was in God's presence, God identified himself as the God of Abraham and Isaac and Jacob. In the woman's story, she was the one asking Jesus if he was greater than Jacob. In Moses' story, the angel of the Lord, who was likely Jesus himself, called out Moses' name two times, but our heroine remains nameless throughout the Scriptures. What seems clear is that although we don't know her name in the story, God does, and his ability to identify her and with her had as strong an impact on her as God saying Moses' name twice had on him. Sometimes our in-between places make us feel hidden or as if we're living in the shadows, but God sees us and calls us by our names when no one else remembers them.

In Exodus 3:7, God explained why he was intervening for his people; he'd heard their cry for help. And I wonder if later, after the woman at the well had some time to process her own conversation with Jesus, she started to realize that God had also heard her cry for help. How many times had she prayed to God to help her? How many times did she petition for someone to take care of her needs? How often had she wondered if God saw her? Just as God could articulate to Moses the misery his people were facing—"I have observed the misery of my people in Egypt" and I have "heard them crying out because of their oppressors" and "I know about their sufferings" and "I have come down to rescue them from the power of the Egyptians" (Ex. 3:7–8)—Jesus named the woman at the well's misery: her five marriages and current relationship.

While God sent Moses to Pharaoh, the woman at the well was sent to the people of her town. While the Israelites needed releasing from Egypt, the people of Shechem needed releasing, too, a release from sin. Feeling trapped in our in-between places is a super-normal experience for many of us. We can barely catch our breath because it's such a tight squeeze in Stuckville. We need to be released. Sometimes we need that liberation to come in a grand gesture, like parting a metaphorical Red Sea, or sometimes in a subtle way, such as making a trip to Shechem on the way through Samaria.

The factor that motivated both Moses and the woman at the well to carry out their missions was knowing that God would be with them—all the way. In Moses' story, God used those exact words: "I will be with you." In fact, he said, "I will certainly be with you" (Ex. 3:12). Could we move forward in confidence from our in-between places if we were not certain Jesus would be with us in our exit? In John 4, the same message is delivered but through the imagery of living water, the ever-present sustaining power of God through Christ. Jesus said, "The water I will give him will become a well of water springing up in him for eternal life" (v. 14). From the sealing of the Holy Spirit to our afterlife with God, he will be with us. How else could we dare step forward?

Like Harriet Tubman, both Moses and the woman in John 4 took their encounters with God back to their people for their salvation and deliverance. Both Moses and the woman at the well needed courage to take their steps of faith. The pinnacle of both stories is God telling Moses he is "I AM" (Ex. 3:14) and the Samaritan woman "I . . . am he" (John 4:26). But the revelation of God's identity and the assurance of his accompaniment were not enough for Moses; he needed a helper, and he needed to know what would happen once he confronted Pharaoh and if the Israelites didn't believe his story. The woman at the well, however, went out alone, in faith.

As a Samaritan woman, she would have been all too familiar with Moses' story because, remember, Samaritans thought Moses was their chief prophet and the coming Messiah. I bet she had Moses' conversation with God memorized. And she was all the better for knowing her faith history, because when her commissioning moment came, she did not hesitate to drop her water jug and go to the people of her town with the gospel news. She didn't need an Aaron to stand by her side the way Moses needed his brother, Aaron, to speak on his behalf (Ex. 4:14). She didn't need her staff to turn into a snake to prove her testimony was true, although that's exactly what Moses needed to get Pharaoh's attention (Ex. 4:1–5). And she didn't need a second sign—her hand changing from leprous to healed with a motion in and out of her coat—the way Moses did in Exodus 4:6–7. She needed only her testimony: "He knew everything I've ever done." And with that, her community would know she was telling the truth. Does anybody need that triple con-firmation like Moses? Yeah, me too. God still worked through Moses, though. But in light of the woman at the well's faith, may we aspire to her level of confidence in God's presence as she ran to tell her people about Jesus. I think the difference is that Moses needed that staff in his hand and a hand in his coat, while her hands were empty.

YOUR WATER JUG IS HEAVY

The grand irony in a comparison of Moses and the woman at the well is that the prophet she so revered and anticipated—Moses—she was now like. While her conversation with Jesus about the mountain of worship was critically important before her faith in Christ, as a Christ follower she was now no longer just an outside participant in religious practice at the temple at Mount Gerizim or the temple in Jerusalem. She *was* the temple now. Now that Jesus was there, the awaited Messiah, she wasn't waiting on Moses. She *was* a Moses. She was supposed to set *her* people free through the empowering of the Holy Spirit because the real Messiah just gave her a testimony.

She left her water jar; having received the living water, she no longer needed the "water" from the well in Samaria. She wouldn't thirst anymore after the Holy Spirit indwelled her body. In fact, according to Jesus, she herself was now the well with the living water springing from inside her.

Like the woman at the well, we inherit the kingdom of God. Ours is a drop-your-water-jug, run-like-a-girl, tell-all-the-people-he-told-you-all-the-things kind of legacy. Called by God himself, we are to pass on the saving knowledge of Jesus to the generations that will follow us as we follow Christ.

That kind of news spread fast because she was willing to share her testimony. I love that she invited people in her town to see for themselves, and that her invitation included an admission about her past. She had done all sorts of things to survive, and Jesus knew them already. But it's her question that brings me hope. She asked the group she was trying to witness to, "He cannot be the Messiah, can he?" (John 4:29 NRSV).

When she dropped her water jug, she emptied her hands of an object that would slow down her running with the gospel message. That causes me to consider, what are our water jugs? What is slowing our pace with the gospel? Her decision embodied enthusiasm for the truth she'd just accepted, the measure of faith in which she received it, and the urgency she felt to share it. Nothing else mattered but taking her salvation to others.

I want to be more like her. I really do. My hands are occupied with goal setting and housekeeping and a whole lot of excuses. With two open hands I could release myself from the extra weight I've been hauling around. Surrendering to our own commissioning as Jesus' disciples means we will have to internalize Jesus as our rescuer. Even if disappointments shatter our dreams like a delicate water jug shatters when it falls to the ground, Jesus can put the pieces back together.

If you're pigeonholed by society's standards of beauty, drop your water jug. If you're overdoing it at work to prove yourself, drop your water jug. If you're covering for someone else's mistakes, drop the water jug. If you're playing house with someone who's not your spouse, drop the water jug. If you're finding all of your own meaning in your kid's achievements, drop your water jug. If your cynicism is protecting you from getting vulnerable, drop the water jug. If your religiosity is preventing real worship, drop the water jug. If you're more comfortable pretending than being authentic, drop the water jug. If you are enslaved to sin, drop the stinkin' water jug. And leave it for Jesus to reconstruct the way he sees fit. Take off running so fast you don't have time to look back at your Shechem. Leave Samaria in the dust of broken pottery. You don't need the water jug anymore because where you're headed, there are streams of living water.

DROP IT ALREADY

Judy Rodriguez is a talented photographer, savvy business-woman, and caring wife and mother. She reminds me of Harriet Tubman, Moses, and the woman at the well. By God's grace, our lives intersected through Polished Ministries. It's hard to miss Judy when she attends a Polished event because her smile lights up a room. Her kindness is contagious. Joy multiplies in her presence because she brings the joy of her salvation to all the spaces she occupies. Without pretense or distraction, she has a way of reminding you that she cares. And without pressure or confusion, she has a way of showing you how God cares.

I'll never forget meeting Judy at a Polished "interest" meeting in Fort Worth, Texas. We didn't have a chapter in Fort Worth yet, but several professional women in the area had reached out, suggesting we gather women together to dream and pray about what it would look like to serve working women there. Judy heard about Polished through social media and showed up to find out what we were all about. I shared the vision and mission: to share the gospel with working women interested in professional and spiritual development while also creating a safe community for Christ followers with a passion for evangelism and discipleship. That's when Judy started to cry. I could see her discreetly sweeping tears to the side of her face and nodding her head with nonverbal amens. Judy is a brave person; she speaks her truth with grace, and you always know where she stands on something. She raised her hand and shared with our group that she had been praying for years that God would show her how to share her faith with some of her sorority sisters, most of whom were now in the workforce or building businesses from home. Judy felt like Polished was the answer to her prayers.

Equipped with tools and resources for effective spiritual conversations, Judy is one of our strongest chapter leaders. The combination of her spiritual discernment, prayer life, and willingness to share has made her an effective change agent in the lives of her friends. It's a treasure to watch her grow in her faith and to grow the kingdom too.

As an organization, we've asked Judy to share parts of her story because her testimony is so strong. Not because she considers evangelism easy breezy; she would tell you it makes her nervous like it does the rest of us. Her testimony is strong because it's so real. When Judy tells you about her experience winning women to Jesus or welcoming them back to church, her starting point is to remind you that she feels inadequate every time she opens her mouth to talk about her relationship with Jesus. The fear of finding the right words never goes away for Judy, but practice has taught her that God is faithful in spite of our inadequacies. As Judy can confirm, putting ourselves out there is unnerving, but she does it anyway. Compelled by Christ's love and empowered by the Holy Spirit, Judy moves around a room greeting guests and hugging acquaintances, then intentionally moves the conversation in a spiritual direction. She'll tell you sometimes the conversations don't go as she hoped, but in spite of that, Judy continues to love people the way God loves us, with gusto.

Continuing as a Polished leader, she has now started a book club and a Bible study and is the definition of a people grower. Just this week she emailed me to say, "I had to share some really exciting news!!! You know how I have been hosting some friends over to do your twelve-week study? Well . . . on Tuesday night one of the ladies stayed late with Evelyn and me. That night my friend Vanessa prayed to accept Jesus in her heart and to be baptized in the Holy Spirit!!!!"

I mention all of this to you because Judy dropped her water jug. In at least one area of her life, I watched it happen. In one hand she was holding fear. Fear of rejection, that her friends would find out just how committed she is to her faith and write her off as crazy. Fear of insufficiency, that fumbling her words and not having all the Bible answers would somehow reflect upon the truth of God's Word. But like Harriet Tubman, she decided that it's freedom or bust for her family and friends. Like Moses, she decided that oppression won't keep her loved ones in captivity. Like the woman at the well, she decided to let her fear go.

The thing is, Moses was a stutterer, the woman at the well was a social misfit, Harriet Tubman was a slave, and Judy Rodriquez was scared. But they went anyway. They were delivered to deliver a deliverance message, and not even their shortcomings stopped their mission work. You don't have to have it all together before you start running in your freedom; go messy early.

Here's to the women ready to drop their old ways for our God-given freedom to run with holy abandon: drop it already.

Discussion Questions

1. Describe a burning-bush moment in your spiritual life.
2. Who has been like a Moses figure in your life? Why?
3. In what area of your life do you need an exodus from sin?
4. Metaphorically speaking, what's your "water jug"?
5. What would it take to drop your water jug?
6. What action steps or accountability steps do you need to help you drop the water jug?

Study Guide

Visit www.katarmstrong.com/theinbetweenplace to download the free study guide. Materials for chapter 9 include

- a chart comparing Moses and the woman at the well
- tips on how to share your faith with others

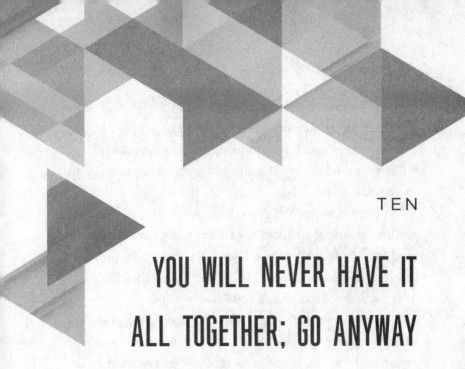

YOU WILL NEVER HAVE IT ALL TOGETHER; GO ANYWAY

Trust God and launch out into the deep.

—FANNIE LOU HAMER

Like the rest of the world, I wasn't prepared for COVID-19. In fact, I would dare say I was in the worst possible shape, emotionally speaking, to face a global pandemic that threatened our existence. As I write this chapter and share with you the internal battle I am fighting, it is not lost on me that hundreds of thousands of people are dead because of the coronavirus disease. As of right now, millions are infected, and *everyone* is being impacted. If not our lives, our livelihoods are at stake. We don't have a vaccine, few of the medical treatments we've tried are successfully helping people with the disease, and if social distancing and sheltering at home don't work, we might run out of ventilators. Not only that, my heart breaks for the millions around the world out of work, practically overnight, as we face our nation's grim economic future.

Lament is now a part of my daily routine because I can't get through one day without news, and no, not from the media machines. I mean a phone call, email, or text from people I love letting me know how COVID-19 is ruining their lives. It's bankrupting us economically *and* emotionally.

My friends who are small-business owners are crippled by shutdowns and furloughs. My friends in corporate America are saying the same thing. Just last week I was on a call with business and ministry leaders in my city, and the owner of a global hotel chain—a grown man, mind you—*wept* over the immediate and devastating impact this is having on the thousands of hourly workers without a way to feed their families. My ministry friends are overwhelmed and often comment on how terribly painful it is to minister to their church members and ministry contacts while they themselves are dealing with the same level of panic and disorientation of grief as those they counsel. My single friends are lamenting loneliness, and my married-with-kids friends are lamenting too much togetherness.

Even if we return to some semblance of normalcy, it will be a new normal none of us was prepared for and most of us don't want. Our old lives are gone, and I haven't had enough time to come to terms with the catastrophic implications.

Naively, I thought I had enough experiences in life to write a whole book about how God changes our stories in our in-between places. Never would I have imagined that something other than my dad's ICU room would be the backdrop for this book. Working a full-time job while crisis home-schooling while self-quarantining, with no end in sight, is my most recent Shechem.

Before COVID-19, I would have told you I was already in a state of emotional crisis. I was at my breaking point. Among other things, I was struggling with burnout. Now, there are different levels of exhaustion. There's "stretched thin," "tired of the daily grind," or "in need of an extended vacation." I was *way* past that, like, two years ago. The fuel of passion that had filled my tank and kept me going for a decade in ministry was suddenly merely fumes.

Burnout reminded me of the time I ran out of gas late one night on a near-empty highway between two small towns. My cell phone battery was dead, the red gas light had been staring at me for miles, and there was no gas station in sight. If you've ever found yourself parking your car on the side of the road and walking to the nearest gas station, you know what I'm talking about. I remember the moment the car started to slow down, even though I was flooring the gas pedal. There was simply nothing left in the tank.

What did your life look like before the pandemic took over? Were you struggling with something already hard enough? Me too.

You may remember my mentioning that, as cofounder, I'm moving into a singular focus with Polished. I've handed the day-to-day operations to an amazing new executive director while I continue to cast a vision, host the podcast, and represent the organization. Guess what? Her first day on the job was our first day of shelter-at-home. Talk about stressful. And anticlimactic. And disappointing. Our ministry had forty more events planned this year, then *poof*! They were all canceled. Training my successor via Zoom was not our plan when we extended the job offer months earlier.

PS: When this is all over, I could go the rest of my life without another Zoom meeting.

Coasting to the side of the road with Polished, sputtering out my last possible strain of energy to train my successor, was only half of my internal battle with burnout. You see, I had a break planned, a three-month glorious sabbatical. I'll admit it; I was fantasizing about time, *alone* time, to connect with God in silence and solitude while my son was in school and my husband was at work. The last time I experienced silence or solitude was long before I googled "how to make your own face masks." What my sabbatical will look like is still TBD, but we know it's not going to meet my expectations.

For the record, the new executive director is amazing. She's the one. Not even a global pandemic can mess with God's timing and plans for Polished. He is working in and through it all; that much is clear. Polished was perfectly positioned to share the gospel with professional women for such a time as this. Record-breaking numbers of women are joining a weekly Polished event online and hearing the good news of Jesus. Which brings me to my point.

Along with my team, I have had to find a way to carry on. In spite of burnout, in spite of our grief over ruined plans, we are taking the gospel forward. It's not because we found the willpower or some reservoir of resilience. No. God's presence, real-time presence, is fueling the imperfect ways the women of Polished and I are choosing to share our testimony of faith with others. When I see the Zoom alert that says, "Your internet connection is unstable," I have to smile at what feels like a metaphor for my current in-between place. Instability is our new reality, but we go with the gospel anyway.

How? For me, it is borrowing the courage of the woman at the well and the other women in the book of John who received revelations from Jesus and then testified about their faith. There is an inescapable pattern in the book of John and, I hope, an inescapable pattern for us too. The woman at the well (John 4), Martha of Bethany (John 11), and Mary Magdalene (John 20) are all featured in John's gospel as outstanding disciples of Jesus. More than that, all three women had the privilege of hearing from Jesus himself that he was the Messiah. Even more shocking, all three of them believed him, and all three went on to share their faith. None of them had it all together, and yet they went with the gospel anyway. Even when *you* don't have it all together, you can contribute to the kingdom of God. At least, that seems to be what John had in mind when he highlighted three outstanding yet imperfect female disciples of Jesus.

THE WOMAN AT THE WELL (JOHN 4)

By all worldly standards, anyone—really *anyone*—would have been a better messenger of the gospel than the woman at the well. Her credibility lessened with every aspect of her personhood. She was the wrong ethnicity, a Samaritan. She was the wrong gender, a woman, who couldn't be trusted in the court of law or used to validate the truth. And she had the wrong lifestyle, divorced and/or widowed many times and living with someone she wasn't married to. But Jesus launched into a rather long discourse with her about deep theological truths the faithful had been wrestling with for centuries.

If you're wrestling with your identity while reading this book, I hope the Holy Spirit grabs your attention. None of the aspects of your personhood that tempt you to doubt yourself missed God's attention when he formed you in your mother's womb. Every single distinction that makes you *you* was intentional on God's part. Rejecting, dismissing, or denying the way you image God could be holding you back from loving him with your all.

Even if we wholeheartedly embrace our divine design as purposeful, we still have to work through ongoing insecurities that make us question, *Am I doing enough? Am I doing what God wants me to do? Am I missing out on his grand plan for me? Why do I feel like an imposter?* I think the woman at the well shows us how to process those natural questions. She was the first to hear Jesus' claim to be "I am." She experienced the thrill of telling others how Jesus changed her life. And she was the first recorded to go and tell her story to win souls for Christ. It seems she was a reluctant preacher, still questioning the encounter herself, but many Samaritans from her town came to believe in Jesus because of her testimony.

Do you consider yourself reluctant when it comes to sharing your faith? Double hand-raises for me too. If you are still questioning your calling or ability, have grace with yourself.

Honestly, I'm not sure we will ever nail that down. What does seem possible is serving God in the *middle* of our in-between places. Because the woman at the well went anyway, you can too. It may look and feel messy. That's okay. Jesus thinks your broken self is worthy of carrying the hope of Jesus to others. In a day and time when believing a woman's testimony was still a struggle for many, Jesus, with undeniable authority, determined a Samaritan woman to be worthy of the gospel message. The Messiah trusted her not only to hear the truth but also to carry it into the world as a herald of salvation. And if Jesus believes women can handle the truth, so should we.

Nike produced a commercial in 2019 titled "Dream Crazier" that reminds me of the female disciples in John's gospel. In Nike's own words, "*Dream Crazier* shines a spotlight on female athletes who have broken barriers, brought people together through their performance and inspired generations of athletes to chase after their dreams."[1] Compiling images of athletic sheroes, Nike accomplished something I hope we can do with the Scriptures. They inspired us to borrow the courage of the women who have gone before us.

Serena Williams, arguably the GOAT (greatest of all time) of tennis, lends her voice to the commercial and says,

> If we show emotion, we're called dramatic. If we want to play against men, we're nuts. And if we dream of equal opportunity, we're delusional. When we stand for something, we're unhinged. When we're too good, there's something wrong with us. And if we get angry, we're hysterical, irrational, or just being crazy.

But a woman running a marathon was crazy. A woman boxing was crazy. A woman dunking, crazy. Coaching an NBA team, crazy. A woman competing in a hijab; changing her sport; landing a double-cork 1080; or winning 23 grand slams, having a baby, and then coming back for more, crazy, crazy, crazy, and crazy.

So if they want to call you crazy, fine. Show them what crazy can do.[2]

Sports are not my thing. Plus, I'm approximately a marathon away from being athletic. I don't run unless I'm being chased, people. Nonetheless, Nike's video fired me up.

Serena's words make me realize you might need to hear plainly that you are not crazy for wanting to serve God. Certainly not because you are a woman. John, Jesus' beloved disciple, made sure to rule out that assumption by highlighting multiple women in his historical biography of Jesus' ministry. The woman at the well is not an outlier. She's not an exception to the rule. She's not a unicorn. She's one of many women in John's gospel who can inspire us to serve God in our in-between places. In John 11, just a few chapters after the woman at the well's encounter with Jesus, John told a story about a woman speaking with Jesus. This time it was Martha of Bethany.

MARTHA OF BETHANY (JOHN 11)

Before reading about Martha for myself, I'd heard only one side of her story. She was the doing-obsessed sister who should have followed her sister's lead. If you've never heard of the Mary/Martha Bible story, here's a short summary: as Jesus was traveling, Martha invited him into her home, and instead of dropping her to-do list, Martha chose chores while her sister, Mary, sat at Jesus' feet to listen to his teaching (Luke 10). What I didn't notice was that there would be no sermons on "Are you are a Mary or a Martha?" had Martha not taken the initiative and welcomed the Jewish rabbi to her home in the first place.

Although Martha incorrectly assumed that serving was the most important thing to do when several out-of-town guests descend upon your home at mealtime, Jesus gently corrected her by reminding her that sitting at his feet, where Mary had chosen to position herself, was the better option. I think Martha took that lesson to heart, because in John 11, when her brother, Lazarus, fell ill and eventually died, she went out to intercept Jesus when he arrived in Bethany. Taking the initiative seemed to be Martha's MO.

Why Jesus didn't leave what he was doing the very moment he heard Lazarus was sick and rush to their side to keep him from dying remains a mystery, especially because Mary, Martha, and Lazarus held such a special place in Jesus' heart. Thankfully, Jesus eventually showed up and said to Martha something as radical as telling the woman at the well that he was the living water. Jesus said, "I am the resurrection and the life. The one who believes in me, even if he dies, will live" (John 11:25). The best part is, he asked Martha if she believed him, and she said yes! Here we have another imperfect woman receiving gospel news and accepting it as truth. In the same way the woman at the well is a Moses figure in her story, Martha of Bethany is a Peter figure in hers.

Her brother's tomb, an in-between place for Martha of Bethany, became a hope-filled space where Jesus changed her story. If we happened to miss the importance of Jesus commissioning the woman at the well, John made sure in his book that we have a second chance to witness another revolutionary female figure making a difference for God. You might experience a full-throttle acceleration in your spiritual life if you model it after the women who have gone before us, like Martha of Bethany. You could be the go-to illustration of what *not* to do in one season of your life and then express radical faith in the next. One doesn't cancel out the other. Based on Martha's example, failing a spiritual test and learning the hard way don't sideline you. It could be exactly what you had to go through to build up your faith. Maybe someone watching your life will be encouraged that you overcame a setback in your faith walk and yet kept going. It was true for Martha, and it was also true for Mary Magdalene.

MARY MAGDALENE (JOHN 20)

Throughout his gospel, John had been priming his readers for a crescendo in John 20. By the time we find Mary Magdalene in the garden tomb searching for Jesus' dead body, it should come as no surprise that she was about to be the first person to see Jesus risen from the dead. She headed to the garden tomb early while it was still dark outside to mourn Jesus' crucifixion.

Her in-between place is more gut-wrenching than all the other stories of deliverance, because on her loss rested the hope of all the world's losses. If Jesus did not conquer death once and for all, it was game over.

This time Jesus didn't need to use any words to proclaim his divinity; his life spoke for itself. While the woman at the well spoke with the Living Water, and Martha of Bethany heard him name himself "the resurrection and the life" (John 11:25), all the resurrected Jesus had to say to Mary was her name (John 20:16). I think it's possible that Jesus said Mary's name as redemption for the woman at the well's nameless-ness. No part of our story is left untouched by his resurrection from the dead. Recognizing her Teacher's voice, Mary leaped toward her Savior, and Jesus had to restrain her enthusiasm with a commissioning service. He asked her to go and tell her brothers that he was alive. This was the most important news ever, and it was a woman who delivered the message. The best part of the story is that she obeyed Jesus. Like the woman at the well, who faithfully told her town about the Savior of the world, or Martha of Bethany, who expressed faith that Jesus could raise the dead, Mary Magdalene told her brothers in the upper room that their in-between place was history.

Mary's story reminds me of Rey, the shero in the Star Wars trilogy. Star Wars spoiler alert: bounce your eyes down to the next paragraph if you haven't seen *The Rise of Skywalker* yet. The last Jedi is a woman, and she defeats evil once and for all by borrowing the courage of the Jedi who have gone before her. And I'm here for it. In the movie, Rey finds herself flat on her back after a long fight. She's come to the end of herself but needs to find the resilience to rise and kill the Sith Lord threatening to destroy the galaxy.

What gets Rey back on her feet? While she lies lifeless on the ground, she starts to hear the voices of Jedi from the past. One by one, each whispers to Rey to get up. For any Star Wars fans, the roll call has the same inspiring impact as Serena's voice-over in "Dream Crazier." Encouraging Rey that they will be with her, stand behind her, and help her rise to the occasion, the Jedi offer her their presence as she fights. I certainly don't get my theology from Star Wars, but the moment is a powerful illustration of someone in an in-between place choosing to get back up one more time and stand her ground.

No description could do the scene justice, but the Sith Lord, the embodiment of evil, condemns Rey as she positions herself to face her enemy. He says, "You are nothing. A scavenger girl is no match for the power in me. I am all the Siths."[3]

I wonder if you've been fighting a battle—something mental, physical, emotional, or spiritual. It took you out, and you feel like you are down for the count. I wonder if you feel like you are nothing. Maybe someone said those cruel words to you, or you feel it through someone's absence or neglect. I wonder if you feel like a scavenger in life, fighting to survive and familiar with the bottom of the barrel. What our Enemy would love for you to believe is that you can't defend yourself, let alone bring hope to our world; that in-between is no place for a comeback story. And it isn't, unless you're relying on the countless testimonies of women whose knees have buckled underneath the pressures of life, and they trust that God's presence will help them rise again.

So what did Rey say in response to the Sith Lord? "And I, I'm *all* the Jedi."[4]

The next time we feel like the wind has been knocked out of our dreams and plans, what if we remember the woman at the well, Martha of Bethany, and Mary Magdalene? What if we picture their weary selves, beaten up by life's hard knocks, and imagine the moment they chose to believe God instead of their circumstances? By God's power, maybe we'd find ourselves ready to go with the gospel.

WOMEN WHO BELIEVE

Why do you think John was relentless with this theme in his gospel account? Could it be that in his providence, God knew you and I would need more than one example of a woman stuck in an in-between place? If you are as thickheaded as I am, maybe the repetition is for us. Maybe we need to see over and over *and over* that we can't do it alone, and we don't have to. Each woman we've zeroed in on found this to be true. The woman at the well needed her community. Martha of Bethany needed her brother and sister. Mary Magdalene needed the disciples in the upper room.

Maybe we have to hear the hard questions all three women asked in their stories. The woman at the well essentially asked, "Is the temple on Mount Gerizim or the one in Jerusalem the right one?" Martha of Bethany asked, "Why didn't you come sooner?" And Mary Magdalene asked, "Where have they put his body?" Boldness and desperation met in their probing questions. Three times we see how Jesus treated women daring to ask their burning questions: he answered.

None of the women had it all together. The woman at the well would have to find a new way to live in light of her salvation but ongoing need to survive. Martha of Bethany would forever be the woman who doubted Jesus' timing, and Mary Magdalene probably never lived down her past of demon possession. But they all went and testified anyway. And we can borrow their courage.

In the middle of COVID-19 and my emotional burnout, I've had to do just that. All my other options were exhausted. Twelve years under my belt, and I finally felt that Polished was solid, but within hours it felt like the rug had been pulled out from under me. Then I thought about the woman at the well and pictured her long, messy hair flying in the air as she ran to her town with a reluctant sermon about her life-changing moment with Jesus. I thought of Martha of Bethany shaking off her reputation as the lady who fumbled a chance to learn from Jesus and instead exhibiting faith. I thought of Mary Magdalene picking up yards of skirt fabric to sprint to the upper room with tear-stained cheeks.

In God's providence, our Polished Sheroes of the Faith series was already planned. We were going to spend weeks talking about our favorite women of the Bible and how to borrow from their courage. When we dreamed about all the female theologians, seminary professors, authors, preachers, ministers, and counselors we would be inviting to be our guest speakers, we had no clue just how much we would need their voices as a "cloud of witnesses" to God's goodness and faithfulness. What we had planned to be in-person events morphed into online Zoom webinars and video recordings, and we were forced to go messy early. Our whole team would tell you, we didn't have it all together during our inaugural weekly webinar, but we went live anyway and ended up reaching over five thousand more women than expected.

You and I have something better than the Jedi of the past. We have Jesus. He is with us till the end and, yes, through the messy middle.

Discussion Questions

1. How did your life change because of COVID-19?
2. What did God teach you during that time?
3. How do you react to unmet expectations?
4. Why do so many of us think we have to have it all together to join God's work?
5. In what ways do you feel unprepared or unqualified to go with the gospel?
6. What would it look like to go anyway?
7. Which women of the Bible inspire you and why?

Study Guide

Visit www.katarmstrong.com/theinbetweenplace to download the free study guide. Materials for chapter 10 include

- a link to the Polished Sheroes of the Faith video series
- Nike commercial "Dream Crazier" link
- *The Rise of Skywalker* link

PART 3 SUMMARY

Together we've studied John 4:16–41, picking up four takeaways that will help us move forward in confidence.

1. No woman is an island. We need Jesus' help in everything. Moving forward in confidence requires releasing our dependency upon anything other than Jesus. Full surrender is truly living.

2. Ask hard questions and accept the truth with courage. Confidence in our future means embracing the divine mystery that is our faith while wholeheartedly devoting our time to understanding God's truth. Holy curiosity is a gift, not a curse. If God has made himself known to us, we would do well to search for answers and enjoy the ways our faith grows in the process.

3. Drop your distractions. Confidence is not the opposite

of doubt; for the Christian, the opposite of confidence is self-sufficiency. God's got you in your in-between place. You can trust him to guide you and use you to set others free too. So drop your water jug already.

4. Go anyway. You will never have it all together. We can borrow the courage of the sheroes in the book of John as we "launch out into the deep."

YOUR HOPE-FILLED SPACES

And they told the woman, "We no longer
believe because of what you said, for we
have heard for ourselves and know that
this really is the Savior of the world."

—JOHN 4:42 HCSB

Trying to muster up enough courage to do a solo hospital visit to see my dad, I phoned my closest friend, my husband, Aaron. I wanted the pep talk of all pep talks as I drove into downtown Dallas. I needed Aaron to tell me something that would get me through. Through the moment, through the season, and through the door to my dad's ICU room. How Aaron understood my plea for help, through my uncontrollable sobs, I am not sure. Practice maybe? He helped me calm down long enough to hear one thing: God is with me. While going into my dad's ICU room felt impossible, overwhelming, and crushing, Aaron calmly reminded me that God would be *with me*. I would not be alone. God would meet me there in my in-between place.

On this side of two years of studying the woman at the well's hope-filled encounter with Jesus, I can see clearly that all the things we've been exploring together are true. When we declare that each step of our journeys has purpose, that is not some trite phrase we embroider on a pillow for the guest bedroom. I know it to be true with all of my being.

Death is always a cruel reminder that God has not yet come back to set all things right, and suicide is never a good thing. At the same time, my Shechem, the ICU room, which the Enemy wanted to use to harm me, has actually been used by God for my good. I'd never hope for you to ever have to face a similar in-between place, but I know that if you do, you will picture Jesus seated at a well in Samaria waiting on a nameless woman for a life-changing conversation.

When I say that even crappy places can be redeemed, I mean it. Redemption, the act of saving us from evil, is possible. We've seen it before when Jesus asked a marginalized woman to disclose her deepest need, and then met it. For me, the aloneness I experienced during the two weeks my dad was in the ICU felt like sinking into the muddy waters of a deep and near-empty well. But God picked me up out of the mire and clay and filled me up with his living water. He can do the same for you.

When I write that Jesus is not done with you yet, you can believe it, because not even a doomed place like Shechem was beyond an epic redo from our Savior. If that is what he can do with Shechem, what could he change for you?

My father's suicide was a culmination of generational sins and curses colliding with his desperation. By all worldly measures, I might be considered doomed to his same choices because I am one of five children, and all five of us have struggled with mental health issues, most of us with substance abuse. Without Jesus stepping into my family history with his life-saving grace, I'd be as good as Shechem. But Jesus is not done with me yet either. God's grace has enabled me to make peace with my past and with my dad's too.

The same is true for you. It's not too late for you to look to your Savior, who is waiting for you with open arms. Years of seminary and Bible-study training have taught me that peace with my past is possible, but this last solo trip to my dad's bedside was a defining moment of my spiritual journey, because my experience confirmed God's truth. This was not theory anymore—I've known the peace that transcends all understanding.

Aaron's reminder that God would be with me felt like my dead batteries were getting a bolt of energy. As my story was unfolding, I was letting Aaron, a very safe person, into my troubles. Although he already knew every twist and turn, every medical update, he let me share with him how this tragedy was affecting me. Like Jesus, Aaron listened well. He let me voice my fears, which was a simple way to help me lessen the weight of the burdens I was trying to carry myself. His comfort, inspired by the God of all comfort, helped me find hope.

As he prayed for me over the phone, memories started

sweeping over me like beach waves rolling onto the shore. Memories of counselors, mentors, and spiritual directors alike teaching me about imaginative prayer, which is imagining Jesus' presence in your current situation. After we hung up the phone, I knew I needed to practice imaginative prayer to walk into my dad's hospital room with confidence.

Trusting the Holy Spirit to direct my thoughts, I pictured Jesus standing in front of the parking spot, waiting for me to arrive at the hospital. There he was, the Palestinian man with scarred hands, motioning me to come close. He waved my car into the spot and helped open my door. I envisioned Jesus holding my hand on the walk across the street into Baylor, a walk I'd made several times at this point. Daydreaming, I stood next to him in the elevator, and then he walked in front of me down the hallways through the double doors until we came to my dad's room. Jesus, I imagined, walked in first. He held the door open for me and welcomed me in. He kissed my father and then knelt next to my dad's bed and put one hand on his beloved Ronald Kent Obenhaus and the other on my shoulder. I saw Jesus' outstretched arms link all three of us. Opening my Bible to John 14, I read aloud, with a cracked voice, Jesus' words to his frightened disciples: "Don't let your heart be troubled. Believe in God; believe also in me" (v. 1).

When the nurse suggested I leave for a few minutes so they could change Dad's bedsheets, I couldn't shake the image of Jesus choosing to stay in the room. Jesus could handle what I could not. As his presence became more real, my thoughts ran wild, and my heart filled with comfort and peace. Aaron was right. The Bible was true. God was, God is, with me. Even in my in-between places. And he's with you too. Yes, even you, even now.

White-knuckling had been my plan before talking to Aaron. I was going to show up and power through, as futile and exhausting as I know that pattern to be. What I wouldn't have given to have already studied the hope the woman at the well found through Jesus. Embracing belonging would have been on my mind earlier, and showing up for myself wouldn't even have been on the table. I'll know better for the next in-between place in my life, because my Savior will come to all of my Samarias and sit with me through the hard conversations.

It's not lost on me that another Samaria is in my future. At some point I'll be at another crossroads. The confusion and fear I've passed through will rear their ugly heads again as I search for God in the middle of the mess. But now I have the story of the woman at the well seared into my heart and mind as a guide. I am equipped, by the truth of God's Word and the power of the Holy Spirit, to walk through another Shechem with my faith intact. What was once an in-between place has become a hope-filled space.

Let's be clear about something. Jesus is the one who can change our in-between places into hope-filled spaces. By *his* power, through *his* life, death, and resurrection, and for *his* glory; Jesus is the Redeemer. But as shocking as it may be, he's chosen you and me to join him in his redemptive work until he comes back to restore everything. Yup, you and me, friend. The women facing the unimaginable, the women living through their greatest nightmares, the women sizing up their lives and feeling like some parts have been a waste. The people

Jesus commissions into redemption work are the women sending out one hundred résumés today because unemployment is their reality, the women reckoning with the news that their spouses have been unfaithful, and the women praying this last round of IVF is a success. Gospel work includes the women scraping by, the women feeling erased on the margins, and the women racking their brains to understand why their children are not living up to their upbringing.

If we don't make peace with our past or find hope in our present or step into our future with confidence, there's no need to drop our water jug. We can just drag it along as we trudge through Shechem, unfazed by Jesus' presence in our Samaria. Or we can drop everything and run. Run like our deepest need has been met, like we know the resurrection from the dead is our future, like soon there will be *no* in-between places.

> They will no longer hunger;
> they will no longer thirst;
> the sun will no longer strike them,
> nor will any heat.
> For the Lamb who is at the center of the throne
> will shepherd them;
> He will guide them to springs of living waters,
> and God will wipe away every tear from their eyes.

—REVELATION 7:16–17 HCSB

ACKNOWLEDGMENTS

Somebody pinch me; is this all real? I'll never get over the inestimable gift it is to steward a message through the written word. Never. The fact that you are reading one of my books is proof that I have the honor of collaborating with a team much smarter and more experienced than I am. It's proof that I am loved and supported by generous and brilliant people who make me better in every way.

I'd like to thank Patty Crowley, my writing coach. She's helped me on two books now, and she's been pacing with me on this long run. With every step she's cheering, encouraging, and coaching me up. Thank you, Patty! I hope we get to work together on many more projects.

Had Debbie Wickwire, my amazing editor, not taken a chance on me, there would be no book to speak of. She has believed in me more than I believe in myself, and I've had to borrow her enthusiasm and expertise throughout this whole process. Debbie, I can't tell you how many times I've expressed to Jana Burson how grateful I am that we were partnered together on this project. Thank you for believing in me.

Jana Burson, my agent, is a fierce prayer warrior and devoted advocate. Her faith in me has been a guardrail when I wanted to jump over the edge. Jana, thank you for steadying me and helping me focus on my faith in the midst of this process. I love working with you! Your faith strengthens mine.

To my marketing team, thank you for helping me get this message out into the world. I can't express how grateful I am to dream together. You've been behind the scenes making sure that readers find the hope of Jesus through *The In-Between Place*, thank you. I couldn't do it without you all.

Jenn McNeil, Julie Breihan, and Meaghan Porter, you are godsends. Thank you for refining these words with such precision and intentionality. You are all greatly appreciated.

Mom, thank you for being my cheerleader. You had your work cut out for you this time as I leaned on your encouragement more than you know. Thank you!

Aaron and Caleb Armstrong, making you proud is a driving force in my life. Thank you for helping me make space in our busy lives to write this message. You have my whole heart.

My side of the family and Aaron's side of the family have been reaching out for months asking about the process and encouraging me with funny GIFs. Thank you for your support; it made a huge difference.

To the Polished family (board, staff, leaders, volunteers, attendees, podcast listeners), thank you for helping me learn how to navigate in-between places. I could do so because of the loving spaces you created for me to flourish.

Without a doubt, I have the very best friends in the world. Lee, Sarah, Jenn, Sharifa, Tiffany, Irina, thank you for catching me every time my faith falls into doubt. Jayme, Crystal, Nika, Joann, Tara, Cheryl and Laura, Michele, Michelle, Kelly, and Kari, you covered me in prayer and I cherish the investment you make in my life.

Many of my brothers in Christ lifted me up by showing interest in the book, and I want to say thanks to Don, Brad, Jonathan, Warren, Ken, and Jason.

Special thanks to my friends Brad and Crystal for inviting me to teach through this material at Dallas Bible Church. Thank you for creating an environment where I love to learn and get to teach.

Special thanks to Kelly Mountjoy and her enthusiasm for this project. You continue to be a lamppost for me, showing me the way forward by simply cheering me on. Thank you!

Special thanks to Tiffany Stein, Dani Ross, and Jonathan Stevens for being early readers and giving me the kind of feedback that has made this book special. Tiffany Stein, I'm not sure I've felt generosity the way I did through your reading of my manuscript. Thank you.

Special thanks to Dr. Sandra Glahn, who has been on this book journey with me from the very beginning. Sandi, I will cherish that screenshot of your first-read feedback forever.

Last, but certainly not least, special thanks to Dr. Jackie Roese, my favorite preacher (besides Aaron, of course) and Lisa Huntsberry. This book was born when Ronnie said, "We are standing in modern-day Samaria. You'll remember it's the setting for the story of the woman at the well. And now we'll hear from Jackie about Dinah's story from Genesis 34." One casual transition statement from our tour guide, Ronnie, about the Holy Land site visit for the day, to our Bible teacher, Jackie Roese, reoriented the way I read the Samaritan woman's conversation with Jesus in John 4. How did I not see it sooner? Both women's stories have Samaria as their setting, and I think there is divine purpose in the places and spaces God revisits in the Scriptures. Lisa, thank you for taking me to Israel. I'll never be the same. Jackie, I love being in your orbit. Thank you for taking so many female preachers into their future by your example.

NOTES

FOREWORD

1. Margaret Roach, "It's Summertime, and the Gardening Should Be Easy, Right?" *New York Times*, July 29, 2020, https://www.nytimes.com/2020/07/29/realestate/garden-summer-august-chores.html.

OUR IN-BETWEEN PLACES

1. Carmen Joy Imes, *Bearing God's Name: Why Sinai Still Matters* (Downers Grove, IL: IVP Academic, 2019), 16. In this book, Imes discusses the concept of "liminality."
2. Spiros Zodhiates, ed., *The Complete Word Study New Testament* (Chattanooga, TN: AMG Publishers, 1992), s.v. "Sychar," 4965. For the sake of clarity, I'll primarily refer to Sychar as Shechem.

CHAPTER 1: EACH STEP OF YOUR JOURNEY HAS PURPOSE

1. Chad Brand et al., eds., *Holman Illustrated Bible Dictionary* (Nashville: Holman Bible Publishers, 2003), s.v. "Judean."

2. Walter A. Elwell et al., eds., *Baker Encyclopedia of the Bible*, vol. 1 (Grand Rapids: Baker Book House, 1988), s.v. "Galilee, Galileans."

3. Elwell, *Baker Encyclopedia of the Bible*, vol. 2, s.v. "Samaria."

4. John D. Barry et al., eds., *The Lexham Bible Dictionary* (Bellingham, WA: Lexham Press, 2016), s.v. "Samaria." Samaria in the Old Testament was a city, and in the New Testament, it was a region. My connection remains the same, since the history of the city/region/people group are all connected and would have been connected in the minds of readers of the Bible.

CHAPTER 2: EVEN CRAPPY PLACES CAN BE REDEEMED

1. Spiros Zodhiates, ed., *The Complete Word Study New Testament* (Chattanooga, TN: AMG Publishers, 1992), s.v. "Sychar," 4965.

2. Melissa Healy, "Suicide Rates for U.S. Teens and Young Adults Are the Highest on Record," *Los Angeles Times*, June 18, 2019, https://www.latimes.com/science/la-sci-suicide-rates-rising-teens-young-adults-20190618-story.html.

3. Ben Witherington, *John's Wisdom: A Commentary on the Fourth Gospel* (Louisville, KY: Westminster John Knox Press, 1995), 115.

CHAPTER 3: JESUS IS NOT DONE WITH YOU YET

1. Robert Alter, *The Art of Biblical Narrative* (New York: Basic Books, 2011), 63, cited in James Bejon, "An Altered Perspective on the Woman at the Well," August 2019, https://www.academia.edu/40181445/An_Altered_Perspective_on_the_Woman_at_the_Well; Carissa Quinn, "Jesus Offers Living Water and . . . Marriage?" *Water of Life* (blog), April 7, 2020, https://bibleproject.com/blog/jesus-offers-living-water-and-marriage/.

2. Ben Witherington, *John's Wisdom: A Commentary on the Fourth Gospel* (Louisville, KY: Westminster John Knox Press, 1995), 118.

3. Bejon, "An Altered Perspective."

4. Brené Brown, *Daring Greatly: How the Courage to Be Vulnerable Transforms the Way We Live, Love, Parent, and Lead* (New York: Avery, 2012), 117–23.

CHAPTER 4: FIND SAFE PEOPLE TO SHARE YOUR STORY WITH

1. *Meet the Fockers*, directed by Jay Roach (Universal City, CA: Universal Pictures/DreamWorks, 2004).

2. "Barna and World Vision Partner to Create Largest Study of Its Kind, Offering New Insights into Millennials and Gen Z Worldwide," PR Newswire, September 10, 2019, https://www.prnewswire.com/news-releases/barna-world-vision-partner-to-create-largest-study-of-its-kind-offering-new-insights-into-millennials-gen-z-worldwide-300915622.html.

3. David G. Benner, *Sacred Companions: The Gift of Spiritual Friendship and Direction* (Downers Grove, IL: InterVarsity Press, 2002), 14–15.

4. Amy Cuddy, "Your Body Language May Shape Who You Are," TEDGlobal, June 2012, https://www.ted.com/talks/amy_cuddy_your_body_language_may_shape_who_you_are.

5. Jack Zenger and Joseph Folkman, "What Great Listeners Actually Do," *Harvard Business Review*, July 14, 2016, https://hbr.org/2016/07/what-great-listeners-actually-do.

6. *West Wing*, "Red Haven's on Fire," season 4, episode 17, directed by Alex Graves, NBC, aired February 26, 2003.

7. Henry Cloud and John Townsend, *Safe People: How to Find Relationships That Are Good for You and Avoid Those That Aren't* (Grand Rapids: Zondervan, 1995), 143.

CHAPTER 5: EMBRACE BELONGING

1. Nika Spaulding, "John Four: Jesus and the Woman at the Well" (paper presented to Dr. Darrell Bock for NT 305 Exegesis of Gospel Narrative, Dallas Theological Seminary, February 2010), 4.

2. Marg Mowczko, "Misogynistic Quotations from Church Fathers and Reformers," *Marg Mowczko* (blog), January 24, 2013, https://margmowczko.com/misogynist-quotes-from-church-fathers/.

3. Tertullian, *De Cultu Feminarum (On the Apparel of Women)*, bk. 1, chap. 1, quoted in Mowczko, "Misogynistic Quotations."

4. Thomas Aquinas, *Summa Theologica*, vol. 1, question 92, art. 1, "Reply to Objection 1," quoted in Mowczko, "Misogynistic Quotations."

5. Martin Luther, *Commentary on Genesis*, chap. 1, sec. 2, pt. 6, v. 27b, para. 1, quoted in Mowczko, "Misogynistic Quotations."

6. Augustine, *De Genesi ad Litteram*, vol. 9, chap. 5, sec. 9, quoted in Mowczko, "Misogynistic Quotations."

7. John Piper and Wayne Grudem, eds., *Recovering Biblical Manhood and Womanhood: A Response to Evangelical Feminism* (Wheaton, IL: Crossway, 2006), 72–73.

8. Mark Driscoll, *On Church Leadership: A Book You Will Actually Read* (Wheaton, IL: Crossway Books, 2008), 48.

9. John MacArthur, interview by Todd Friel (panel discussion, Truth Matters Conference at Grace Community Church, Sun Valley, California, October 18, 2019), https://www.youtube.com/watch?v=NeNKHqpBcgc.

10. Spaulding, "John Four," 2.

11. Mishnah Niddah 4:1.

12. Spaulding, "John Four," 2.

13. Spaulding, "John Four," 2.

14. Ben Witherington, *John's Wisdom: A Commentary on the Fourth Gospel* (Louisville, KY: Westminster John Knox Press, 1995), 121.

15. Witherington, *John's Wisdom*, 125.
16. Gail R. O'Day, "Gospel of John," in Carol A. Newsom, Sharon H. Ringe, and Jacqueline E. Lapsley, eds., *Women's Bible Commentary*, 20th anniv. ed. (Louisville, KY: Westminster John Knox Press, 2012), 521.
17. O'Day, "Gospel of John," 521.
18. Brené Brown, *The Gifts of Imperfection: Let Go of Who You Think You're Supposed to Be and Embrace Who You Are* (Center City, MN: Hazelden Publishing, 2010), 25.
19. Brown, *Gifts of Imperfection*, 26.

CHAPTER 6: STOP SHOWING UP FOR YOURSELF

1. Leland Ryken, *How to Read the Bible as Literature and Get More out of It* (Grand Rapids: Zondervan, 1984), 95.
2. Biblica.com, s.v. "Intro to Jeremiah," https://www.biblica.com/resources/scholar-notes/niv-study-bible/intro-to-jeremiah/.
3. Cory Asbury, Caleb Culver, and Ran Jackson, "Reckless Love," Bethel Music, 2017, https://bethelmusic.com/chords-and-lyrics/reckless-love/.

CHAPTER 7: NO WOMAN IS AN ISLAND

1. Lynn Cohick, "The 'Woman at the Well': Was the Samaritan Woman Really an Adulteress?" in Sandra Glahn, ed., *Vindicating the Vixens: Revisiting Sexualized, Vilified and Marginalized Women of the Bible* (Grand Rapids: Kregel Academic, 2017), 250.
2. Cohick, "The 'Woman at the Well,'" 250.
3. Cohick, "The 'Woman at the Well,'" 251.
4. Cohick, "The 'Woman at the Well,'" 251.
5. Janeth N. Day, "The Woman at the Well: Interpretation of John 4:1–42 in Retrospect and Prospect" (PhD diss., Baylor University, 1999), 219.

6. Day, "The Woman at the Well."

7. *Little Women*, directed by Greta Gerwig, screenplay by Greta Gerwig (Culver City, CA: Columbia Pictures, 2019).

CHAPTER 8: BE BRAVE ENOUGH TO ASK HARD QUESTIONS AND ACCEPT THE TRUTH

1. Wendy Murray Zoba, "The Grandmother of Us All," *Christianity Today*, September 16, 1996, https://www.christianitytoday.com/ct/1996/september16/6ta044.html.

2. All information about Henrietta Mears in this chapter is taken from Richard J. Leyda, "Henrietta Cornelia Mears," Biola University, https://www.biola.edu/talbot/ce20/database/henrietta-cornelia-mears.

3. Leyda, "Henrietta Cornelia Mears."

4. "Passion Conferences, OneDay 2000, Shelby Farms, TN," Facebook post, May 20, 2017, https://www.facebook.com/Passion268/photos/a.498514484921/10156195691799922/?type=1&theater.

5. Walter A. Elwell et al., eds., *Baker Encyclopedia of the Bible*, vol. 2, eds. W. A. Elwell and B. J. Beitzel (Grand Rapids: Baker Book House, 1988), s.v. "Samaria."

6. *Baker Encyclopedia*, s.v. "Samaria."

7. Dr. Thomas L. Constable, "Notes on John," Plano Bible Chapel, 2020, https://planobiblechapel.org/tcon/notes/pdf/john.pdf, 126–27.

CHAPTER 9: DROP YOUR DISTRACTIONS

1. "Harriet Tubman," in "Judgment Day," pt. 4 of Africans in America, PBS, https://www.pbs.org/wgbh/aia/part4/4p1535.html.

2. "Harriet Tubman: The Moses of Her People," *Christianity*

Today, https://www.christianitytoday.com/history/people/activists/harriet-tubman.html.

3. Debra Michals, ed., "Harriet Tubman," National Women's History Museum, 2015, https://www.womenshistory.org/education-resources/biographies/harriet-tubman.

4. *Encylopaedia Britannica*, s.v. "Harriet Tubman," March 6, 2020, https://www.britannica.com/biography/Harriet-Tubman.

5. "Harriet Tubman," PBS.

6. Tremper Longman III and Raymond B. Dillard, *An Introduction to the Old Testament*, 2nd ed. (Grand Rapids: Zondervan, 2006), 70.

7. Nyasha Junior, "Exodus," in Carol A. Newsom, Sharon H. Ringe, and Jacqueline E. Lapsley, eds., *Women's Bible Commentary*, 20th anniv. ed. (Louisville, KY: Westminster John Knox Press, 2012), 59.

CHAPTER 10: YOU WILL NEVER HAVE IT ALL TOGETHER; GO ANYWAY

1. "Dream Crazier," Nike News, https://news.nike.com/featured_video/dream-crazier.

2. Tim Nudd, "Nike Takes Oscars by Storm with 'Dream Crazier,' Narrated by Serena Williams," MUSE by Clio, February 24, 2019, https://musebycl.io/sports/nike-takes-oscars-storm-dream-crazier-narrated-serena-williams.

3. *Star Wars: The Rise of Skywalker*, directed by J. J. Abrams (San Francisco: Lucasfilms Ltd., 2019).

4. *Star Wars: The Rise of Skywalker*.

ABOUT THE AUTHOR

KAT ARMSTRONG has been emboldening women to be all in for Jesus for twenty years as a speaker, Bible teacher, author, and podcast host. As cofounder of the Polished Network, a nonprofit connecting and gathering professional women to navigate career and explore faith, her mission is to create holy curiosity. Kat holds a master of Christian education from Dallas Theological Seminary. She and her husband, Aaron, have been married for eighteen years and live in Dallas, Texas, with their son, Caleb. They attend Dallas Bible Church, where Aaron serves as the lead pastor.

www.katarmstrong.com